The Ultimate Guide to 209 Things to Do When You Retire

Kate Rian

Copyright © 2023 by Kate Rian

All rights reserved. No part of this publication may be reproduced, stored or transmitted in any form or by any means, electronic, mechanical, photocopying, recording, scanning, or otherwise without written permission from the publisher. It is illegal to copy this book, post it to a website, or distribute it by any other means without permission. Publisher: thadypublishing@gmail.com

First Edition 2023

Table of Contents

Congratulations you're officially retired! 9

Themed activity trips: 14

Cooking Holiday 14

Wildlife Photography Safari 16

Fishing Holiday 18

Bridge weekends 20

Tennis camp weeks 23

Golfing holidays 24

Yoga Retreats 26

Scuba Diving Holiday 28

Pottery Holiday 30

Wine Tasting Tour 31

Gardening Retreat 33

Adrenaline junkie ideas 36

    Surfing weeks 36

    Skiing/Snowboarding Holiday 37

    Rock Climbing Trip 39

    Sailing Holiday 41

    Cycling Holiday 42

    Hiking/Backpacking Holiday 44

Unleash your creativity 46

    Drawing 46

    Painting 48

    Photography 49

    Drone Photography 51

    Sculpting 52

    Leatherworking 54

    Metalworking 56

    Origami 58

    Pottery 59

    Calligraphy 60

Knitting 62

Digital Art 64

Sewing 65

Jewelry Making 67

Embroidery 68

Quilting 70

Screen Printing 71

Glass Blowing 73

Woodworking 74

Woodturning 76

Car Restoration 77

Model Building 78

Photography 80

Films 81

Short films 82

Documentaries 84

Writing 86

Publish a memoir 86

Write a children's picture book 90

Write a poetry book 95

Write a letter to your local newspaper 96

Write a press release to help a local business 98

Write a short story 101

Start a blog 102

Write a screenplay 103

Start a journal 104

Songwriting 105

Vacation adventures 107

  USA 107

  UK 119

  Europe 128

  Canada 132

  Australia & NZ 136

  South America 140

Dance classes 144

  Ballet 144

    Hip-Hop 144

    Salsa 145

    Ballroom Dancing 145

    Belly Dancing 146

    Zumba 146

    Tap Dancing 147

    Jazz 147

    Pole Dancing 148

    Line Dancing 148

Music 150

    Learn to play an instrument 151

    Start singing lessons 157

    Become a rockstar 158

    Join an orchestra 160

    Join a choir 162

    Join a local folk group 164

    Join a musical society 166

Cooking & food 183

    Cooking classes 183

Wine tasting 188

Travel for food 190

Home brewing 195

Animals 197

Adopt an animal 197

Train a guide dog puppy 201

Volunteer at local animal shelter 202

Take horseback riding lessons 204

Get political 206

Further education & getting on stage 209

Local college courses 209

Languages 210

Conferences 214

Acting 221

Map your family tree 227

Entrepreneurship adventures 241

Online business ideas 242

You're a legend! 253

Congratulations you're officially retired!

Who said retirement is about knitting, daytime TV, and too early bird specials? That's right, nobody who has read this book! Welcome, my fellow retiree, to your new life! Retirement is here and with it comes a world of possibilities! You've earned every wrinkle, each silver hair, and now it's time to put them to good use.

Don't you just love the sound of 'retirement'? It's like a sigh of relief after a long day's work. It's time to swap business meetings for tennis matches, and lunch at your desk for a picnic in the park.

And remember, it's always 5 o'clock somewhere - so why not start that wine tasting course you've always fancied? First off, let's get one thing straight: retirement is not the end. Oh, no, no, no! It's the beginning, the start of the grandest adventure yet! You might be hanging up your work boots, but you're lacing up your dancing shoes, your hiking boots, or perhaps those shiny new sneakers for tennis.

Remember those sailing lessons you always wanted but never had the time for? Well, guess what? Now's the time to set sail on new adventures, and don't worry if you don't know your port from your starboard - that's part of the fun!

Ever dreamt of strumming your guitar on a stage, the crowd cheering your name? Well, who's stopping you now? Remember, lots of rock stars from the 60's and 70's are still rocking well into their seventies and beyond. If they can do it, so can you!

But what if you've never done anything like that before? To which I say, that's fantastic! It's the first-timers, the beginners, the 'I've-never-done-this-before-but-I'll-give-it-a-go' adventurers who have the most fun.

Is there a novel brewing inside you that you've been dreaming of writing "one day"? Unleash it! Your life story could be the next big thing. And if you end up writing about alien abduction or time-traveling dinosaurs, so be it!

This first chapter is an invitation to embrace the unexpected, to throw caution to the wind (but not your back - remember to bend your knees!).

It's time to dive headfirst into the smorgasbord of opportunities that await you. It's time to fill your life with more stories, more laughs, and more 'I can't believe I just did that!' moments.

From gardening and fishing to choir singing and salsa dancing, this book is brimming with ideas to fill your days with fun, laughter, and a dash of the unexpected. Because let's face it, who wants to sit in a rocking chair when you can be rocking the stage, the dance floor, or the high seas?

So whether you fancy becoming a wildlife photographer, an author, a globetrotter, an opera sensation, a surfer, or a gardener extraordinaire, this book has got you covered.

Retirement isn't about fading into the background; it's about stepping into the spotlight and living your life in full technicolor. Buckle up, because it's going to be a wild, hilarious, and utterly unforgettable ride! Welcome to retirement - your adventure starts here!

Themed activity trips:
Cooking Holiday

Ever burned toast or have major issues boiling an egg? Fear not! A cooking holiday is here to save your kitchen disasters and turn you into a culinary wizard. It's designed for all levels - from those who struggle to boil an egg, to seasoned home chefs looking for new recipes to master. During a cooking holiday, you'll learn how to prepare local dishes from professional chefs, often using fresh ingredients from local markets or even straight from a garden.

One useful tip is to bring a notebook to jot down recipes, techniques, and tips from your cooking lessons.

Don't be afraid to ask questions or make mistakes. Not only will you upgrade your kitchen skills and learn to make delicious dishes, but you'll also get a taste (literally!) of the local culture.

Plus, cooking is a creative and relaxing activity that can also be a great social experience. So, if you're keen to swap your kitchen calamities for culinary conquests, a cooking holiday could be just the recipe you need!

Wildlife Photography Safari

Have you ever dreamed of being a world renowned wildlife photographer? Then a wildlife photography safari might just be for you! It's open to all, from those whose camera is still in auto mode, to seasoned photographers looking to capture the perfect lion's yawn.

On a safari, you can expect guided tours through stunning wildlife reserves, photography lessons from professionals, and the chance to see and photograph amazing animals in their natural habitat.

A useful tip is to bring plenty of memory cards. And don't forget lots of batteries - you don't want to miss the perfect shot because you ran out of storage or power. Also, remember to be patient. Wildlife photography often involves waiting for the right moment, which can take time.

You'll learn new photography skills, get to experience the thrill of seeing wild animals up close, and have the opportunity to capture these moments in your own unique way.

Plus, you'll likely make new friends who share your love for photography and wildlife.

Fishing Holiday

Ever found yourself exaggerating the size of the "one that got away"? Well, a fishing holiday might just turn your fishy fables into reality. It's a holiday that's perfect for everyone - from those who've never held a fishing rod to seasoned anglers looking for their next big catch.

On a fishing holiday, you can expect to spend time at lakes, rivers, or even out at sea, casting your line and waiting for a bite. You might also learn new fishing techniques, depending on the type of fishing offered.

A useful tip is to bring all-weather clothing. It can get cold sitting by the water, and rain can often make the fish bite.

Remember, patience is key - fish don't always bite immediately, so be prepared to wait for that thrilling tug on the line. It's also a chance to relax, spend time in nature, and learn or hone a fun new skill. There's also the thrill of the catch, and the satisfaction of cooking and eating your own freshly caught fish.

Plus, you'll have the opportunity to meet fellow fishing enthusiasts and swap stories (and maybe even some friendly exaggerations) about the one that got away.

So, if you're ready to reel in some fun, a fishing holiday might be just the catch you need!

Bridge weekends

We can't all win millions on poker, but you can do the next best thing and play bridge!

Bridge cards holidays are the perfect way to exercise your brain while you kick back and relax. It's an ideal activity for anyone, regardless of age and experience, who enjoys strategy, friendly competition, and the chance to meet like-minded people. During these holidays, you can expect daily bridge sessions, learning new tactics, and the thrill of competition in a friendly environment.

Don't worry if you're a beginner; everyone was once! Just remember to keep an open mind, be ready to learn, and definitely don't forget to have fun.

During the weekend, you can expect to play several rounds of Bridge, often with different partners and opponents, which helps you learn different strategies and styles of play. It's a great idea to bring a notebook to jot down any new techniques or tips you learn.

The atmosphere at these weekends is friendly and welcoming, and there are often tutors on hand to help explain the rules and give advice on improving your game. Be open to their suggestions and willing to try new strategies.

Taking part in a bridge weekend has many benefits. It's a fun way to make new friends who share your interest in the game.

Plus, as Bridge requires concentration and strategic thinking, it's a good mental workout too. The benefits are plentiful, from sharpening your memory and problem-solving skills to creating a sense of community. So go ahead and deal yourself in - it's your move!"

Tennis camp weeks

Who said holidays are only for lying on a beach sipping lemonade? They're also for running around a tennis court and sweating buckets! Tennis holidays are designed for everyone, from beginners who have never held a racket before, to experienced players who want to perfect their serve. On a tennis holiday, you can expect professional coaching sessions, friendly matches with other guests, and lots of time on the court to practice your skills.

One useful tip is to bring very comfortable clothes and shoes, as you'll be spending a few hours each day on court.

And don't forget sunscreen if you'll be playing outdoors. Be ready to learn - the coaches are there to help you improve. Tennis is a great form of exercise, so you'll be keeping fit while having a blast. So, whether you're a seasoned player or a complete beginner, a tennis holiday could be a smashing good time!

Golfing holidays

Who knew that chasing a little white ball around a large field could be so much fun? Golf holidays are the perfect pastime for anyone who enjoys long walks, impeccable lawns, and the challenge of getting a tiny ball into a slightly larger hole. It's the thrill of the chase!

Whether you're a budding golf superstar or a novice still figuring out which end of the club to hold, a golf holiday has something for you. Expect crisp early mornings on the green, intense putting practice, and the sweet sound of 'fore!' ringing in your ears.

Some useful tips? Don't forget your sunblock, make sure your swing isn't rusty, and remember, it's just a game. As for the benefits, besides the obvious exercise and skill improvement, you'll develop patience, a competitive spirit, and possibly, a strange fascination with argyle patterns!"

Also remember to bring comfortable clothing and shoes, as you'll be standing and walking a lot. Don't forget your golf clubs, although many places offer rentals if you prefer to travel light.

Golf is a super way to relax and take your mind off everyday stress. Plus, it's a social sport, so you'll have the chance to meet other golfers and make new friends. So, whether you're a golf pro or a curious beginner, a golfing holiday could be the perfect break for you.

Yoga Retreats

Imagine this: you're attempting the warrior pose on a beach while a gentle sea breeze ruffles your hair. Yes, we're talking about yoga holidays, the ideal escape for anyone who wants to say 'namaste' to their stress and 'hello' to inner peace.

Whether you're a yogi master who can bend like a pretzel or a beginner who still confuses 'downward dog' with an actual pet, yoga holidays cater to all.

Expect sunrise meditations, rejuvenating asanas, and the beautiful balance between mindfulness and movement.

The benefits? You get to stretch your body, expand your mind, and if you engage in some home brewing (after a class, of course), you might find the ritual of preparing your own brew can be just as calming and meditative as your yoga practice.

So roll up your mat, pack your bags, and get ready to find your zen!"

A useful tip for a yoga retreat is to bring very comfortable clothing.

Also, while there might be a schedule, it's usually flexible, so you can participate in as much or as little as you want. It's also a chance to deepen your yoga practice and learn new techniques. You can take a break from daily life, relax, and focus on your well-being.

Plus, you'll likely meet a group of like-minded people who share your interest in yoga. So, if you're looking for a holiday that's relaxing, healthy, and a little bit different, a yoga retreat could be just the ticket!

Scuba Diving Holiday

Ever dreamed of exploring the underwater world? If so, a scuba diving holiday would be perfect for you!

It's suitable for everyone, from beginners who've never dived before, to experienced divers looking for new adventures.

On a scuba diving holiday, you can expect to dive in beautiful locations, see colorful marine life, and depending on your level, you might even take scuba lessons or earn a diving certification.

A useful tip for a scuba diving holiday is to bring your own mask, snorkel, and fins if you have them, as they can be more comfortable when they're custom-fitted. Also, it's important to listen to your instructor or dive guide and always prioritize safety.

There are many benefits to a scuba diving holiday.

You get to explore the fascinating underwater world and see incredible marine life up close. The underwater environment can also be incredibly peaceful. Plus, scuba diving is a fun and exciting way to stay active on your holiday.

Pottery Holiday

Pottery holidays are becoming really popular around the world. Suitable for all levels - from those who've never touched clay to experienced potters looking to refine their skills - it's a creative break like no other.

On a pottery holiday, you can expect to learn various techniques, such as wheel throwing and hand building, guided by professional potters.

A useful tip is to bring clothes you don't mind getting a little dirty - clay can be messy. Also, be patient and kind to yourself; it takes time to master the art of pottery.

You'll get to unleash your creativity, learn a new skill, and maybe even make your own dishes or decorative items. Pottery is also a relaxing and therapeutic activity, providing a great way to unwind, and get all your Christmas gifts made too!

Wine Tasting Tour

Ever found yourself nodding along when someone mentions "tannins" and "bouquets", while you're just thinking, "Mmm, this is good wine"?

A wine tasting tour could be the perfect way to put a cork in your wine confusion.

This type of holiday is open to everyone, whether you're a wine novice who can't tell a Merlot from a Malbec, or a seasoned connoisseur looking to expand your palate. Expect to visit vineyards, learn about the winemaking process, and sample lots of different types of wines.

A useful tip for wine tasting is to not feel pressured to finish every glass. It's totally acceptable to spit out wine after tasting (in fact, it's common practice at many tastings). Drink lots of water and eat food throughout the day to avoid becoming tipsy. You'll get to learn about different types of wine and how they're made, develop your palate, and discover new favorites.

Plus, you'll get to explore beautiful vineyards and wineries, often in stunning locations. It's also a great social activity, perfect for meeting fellow wine enthusiasts. So, if you're ready to swap your wine confusion for connoisseurship, a wine tasting tour could be just the ticket!

Gardening Retreat

Love plants, but not entirely sure if they love you back? Ever mistaken a weed for a rare plant or accidentally pruned a plant to oblivion?

An educational gardening retreat is just the solution to help your green thumb truly earn its name.

This holiday is perfect for all levels - from folks who've only ever owned plastic plants, to experienced gardeners looking to deepen their knowledge. At an educational gardening retreat, you can expect to learn about various types of plants, gardening techniques, and how to care for your garden.

A useful tip is to bring a notebook and pen to jot down all the golden nuggets of gardening wisdom. Be ready to get your hands dirty! Not only will you learn valuable gardening skills, but you'll also get to spend time outdoors, which can be incredibly relaxing and rejuvenating. Gardening can be a very rewarding hobby. Plus, you'll meet other plant enthusiasts and learn from their experiences.

So, if you're ready to transform your brown thumb into a green one, an educational gardening retreat could be the seed you need to sow!

Adrenaline junkie ideas
Surfing weeks

Cowabunga! Now, that's a word you might want to get familiar with because we're diving into the thrilling world of surfing holidays. Are you someone who can't resist the call of the waves or perhaps someone who just wants to look cool walking along the beach with a surfboard? Then this is for you.

Expect early mornings chasing the best (or the smallest, if you're a beginner) waves, afternoons practicing your balance, and evenings sharing tales of 'the one that got away.' Remember to pack a high SPF sunscreen and always respect the ocean.

Remember, everyone falls off their board a lot at first - it's all part of the learning process! Surfing is also a great full-body workout and a wonderful way to connect with nature. You'll also meet new people who are learning just like you. So, if you've ever dreamed of riding the waves, a beginners surfing holiday could be the perfect way to get started!

Skiing/Snowboarding Holiday

Tired of tumbling down the bunny slope while toddlers zoom past you? A skiing or snowboarding holiday might be just what you need to transform from newbie to pro.

These holidays cater to all levels - from beginners who struggle to stay upright, to advanced riders carving up the black runs.

Expect to spend your days on the slopes under the guidance of experienced instructors, improving your skills and maybe even trying out some new tricks.

A useful tip is to invest in good quality gear, or at least make sure the rented equipment fits well – this can make a world of difference to your comfort and performance. Remember to start slow and take lessons if you're a beginner. Safety is paramount.

Aside from learning a new skill or advancing your current abilities, you'll get to soak up the breathtaking mountain scenery and enjoy the exhilarating feeling of sliding down the slopes.

Plus, it's a fantastic workout, and the après-ski scene offers a fun social environment to unwind and share stories of the day's adventures. So, get ready to leave those toddlers in the dust and embrace your inner winter sports enthusiast with a skiing or snowboarding holiday!

Rock Climbing Trip

If you've spent more time admiring the rock wall at the gym than actually climbing it, a rock climbing holiday might just be the push you need to reach new heights. From beginners who've only climbed the stairs to seasoned pros used to scaling towering cliffs, this holiday offers something for everyone.

Expect to strap into a harness and challenge yourself on a variety of climbing routes, guided by experienced instructors who'll teach you the ropes (quite literally).

A useful tip is to wear comfortable clothing you can move in. Don't be disheartened if you don't reach the top right away - climbing is as much about strategy and perseverance as it is about strength.

Not only will you develop your physical strength and endurance, but you'll also work on your problem-solving skills as you navigate the best path up the rock. It's an adrenaline-filled sport that offers a sense of accomplishment like no other when you reach the top. Plus, it's a great way to meet like-minded adventurers and enjoy some truly stunning views.

So, strap on your harness, chalk up your hands, and get ready to conquer those crags on a rock climbing holiday!

Sailing Holiday

Who needs a car when you've got the wind, right? A sailing holiday is like taking a road trip on the sea; instead of asphalt, you've got the open water. It's perfect for beginners or old salts alike - you don't need a ton of experience to enjoy it.

On this type of holiday, you can expect beautiful sunrises, salty sea air, and a newfound appreciation for seagulls. Remember to bring your sunscreen, a good book, and of course, your adventurous spirit.

Don't worry if you can't tell port from starboard; there's always a chance to learn as you go.

The benefits? You get to unplug from the daily grind, learn new skills and connect with nature. So, hoist the sails, matey, an adventure awaits you!

Cycling Holiday

Remember the freedom and joy of cycling around your neighborhood as a kid? A cycling holiday is here to remind you that bikes aren't just for people to commute into work on! Suitable for all levels - from those who can barely keep their balance to avid cyclists looking for their next challenge - a cycling holiday takes you on a journey like no other.

Expect to pedal your way through scenic landscapes, quaint villages, and bustling cities, guided by local experts who know the best paths to take.

A useful tip for a cycling holiday is to pack light but don't forget essentials like a good sunscreen, comfortable cycling clothes, and a reusable water bottle to keep yourself hydrated. And, remember, it's not a race; take your time and enjoy the ride.

You can explore new places at a slower pace, stay active and enjoy the great outdoors. You'll get to connect with local cultures in a unique way and meet fellow cycling enthusiasts. So, dust off that helmet, oil that chain, and get ready to pedal your way to an unforgettable adventure on your next cycling holiday!

Hiking/Backpacking Holiday

Do you find yourself daydreaming about wandering through lush forests, scaling majestic mountains, or exploring dramatic coastlines? Then a hiking or backpacking holiday may just be the adventure you're longing for. This type of holiday is perfect for every level of hiker - from the occasional park stroller to the seasoned mountain trekker.

Expect to lace up your boots each day and traverse diverse terrains, led by expert guides who can show you amazing trails and breathtaking viewpoints.

Remember to pack essentials such as a comfortable of hiking boots, a waterproof jacket, and plenty of water.

And don't forget, it's the journey that matters – so have fun and soak in the scenery. Hiking is great to improve your fitness while immersing yourself in the beauty of nature.

You'll get a sense of accomplishment with every step, especially when you reach a peak or complete a challenging trail. Plus, it's a great way to disconnect from everyday life and connect with fellow nature lovers. So, pull up your socks, strap on your pack, and step into the great outdoors on your next hiking or backpacking holiday!

Unleash your creativity
Drawing

Drawing: It's not just for people who can turn a squiggly line into a masterpiece! Whether you've got the hand of a surgeon or the coordination of a jellyfish on roller skates, learning to draw can be an exciting journey for anyone. You can expect some challenges, from those pesky perspectives to mastering the art of shadow and light, but the joy of seeing your ideas come to life on paper is unparalleled. A useful tip is to start with simple shapes, and remember, practice is your best friend. Drawing enhances your creativity, helps improve hand-eye coordination, and it's also a fantastic stress reliever.

There are lots of free drawing tutorials online which can help you learn different techniques and styles. As you gain more experience, you can experiment with different materials, like colored pencils, markers, or even digital art tools.

The benefits of drawing as a hobby are numerous. It can help you relax and improve your observation skills! Plus, it's a portable hobby - you can take your sketchbook and pencils with you wherever you go. Many online platforms offer classes, or you can look for local community classes. You'll learn basic techniques and gradually move to more complex drawings. So grab some paper, a pencil, and get ready to make your mark... literally!

Painting

Buckle up, Picasso in the making! Painting is not just for people with fancy berets and a mysterious gaze. It's for anyone who's ever looked at a blank canvas and thought, 'I could throw some color on that!' Expect splashes of excitement, strokes of challenge, and blotches of fun.

Remember, it's not about the destination, but the journey of creating something uniquely yours. A helpful tip is to let go of perfection, experiment with colors, and embrace happy little accidents (they often lead to the best masterpieces!). Painting benefits you in ways you might not expect - it enhances creativity, improves focus and patience, and is a great stress buster.

Practice regularly, be patient with yourself, and remember that every artist has their unique style.

Over time, you'll see improvement and gain more confidence. The benefits of painting as a hobby include stress relief, improved creativity, and a sense of accomplishment when you complete a piece. Plus, you'll create beautiful artwork that you can hang on the wall in your home. So get ready, grab those brushes, and let your inner artist out to play!

Photography

Ever dreamed of being a paparazzi? Well, starting photography as a hobby is a fantastic way to capture the world around you. To begin, you'll need a camera.

This could be a digital camera, a film camera, or even your smartphone. Spend some time learning about your camera and its settings. Then, start taking pictures! You can photograph anything that catches your eye - people, landscapes, animals, or small details. Try taking photos at different times of the day and from different angles to see how it changes the image. You'll find lots of free online lessons and photography blogs, to help you learn and improve. The benefits of photography are many. It can help to improve your observation and concentration skills, and provides a creative outlet. Plus, it's a flexible hobby that you can do almost anywhere, and it can be really satisfying to capture a beautiful moment or scene. You can even work towards holding a photography exhibition!

Drone Photography

If you're keen on snapping jaw-dropping photos from a vantage point only birds usually enjoy, then drone photography is for you. To begin, you'll need a drone with a good quality camera. Start by learning how to safely operate your drone, understanding its controls, and the research where and when you can fly. Most countries have laws around this. It's also important to learn about weather conditions as they can affect your drone's performance. Once you've got the hang of flying, you can start taking photos or videos. Drones allow you to capture images from high above, giving you unique perspectives that you couldn't get otherwise.

There are online communities and resources to help you improve your skills and share your work. The benefits of drone photography are many. It can be a thrilling hobby that combines technology with creativity. It allows you to capture stunning landscapes, cityscapes, and even events like weddings or sports from a completely new angle. Plus, it can give you a deeper appreciation for the beauty of your surroundings.

Sculpting

Even if you're not an Italian called Leonardo, starting sculpting as a hobby is a wonderful way to express yourself in three dimensions.

To begin, you'll need some sculpting clay, which is easy to buy at a local arts and crafts store. You'll also need some basic sculpting tools, but even simple household items like a butter knife or a toothpick can work to start. Begin by molding the clay into simple shapes, like spheres or cubes, to get the feel of the material. Then, let your imagination run wild! You can create anything from abstract shapes to detailed figures. There are many online tutorials and local classes that can help you learn and improve. The benefits of sculpting are numerous. It's a great way to improve your hand-eye coordination, it can be a relaxing and therapeutic activity, and it allows you to bring your ideas to life in a tangible form. Plus, you'll create unique pieces of art that can be used as decoration or given as gifts.

Leatherworking

If you have a hankering for crafting, a love for timeless materials, and a certain stubbornness that mirrors the resilience of leather, then leatherworking is the hobby for you. Brace yourself for a journey that's equal parts challenging and rewarding. Leather isn't the most forgiving medium, but oh boy, when you get it right, it's worth all the effort. To start leatherworking as a hobby, you'll need some basic tools like a cutting mat, a rotary cutter or utility knife, a ruler, and leather needles. You'll also need some leather from a local craft store or online shop. Start by learning how to cut leather and sew pieces together. You might begin with a simple project like a keychain or a small pouch.

There are many free tutorials and patterns online to help guide you. Over time, you can try more complex projects. A pro tip for beginners: start with a small project like a wallet or keychain before moving on to larger items like bags or belts. Plus, who knows? Your handcrafted leather goods might just become the talk of the town!

Metalworking

Get ready to channel your inner blacksmith, minus the gruff beard and medieval attire!" If you've ever been fascinated by the idea of transforming a hunk of cold, hard metal into something elegant and useful, then metalworking might just be the craft for you.

This hobby is for anyone with a dash of patience, a pinch of creativity, and a healthy respect for the power of a good hammer. When starting, expect a fair share of 'clangs' and 'clanks', as you learn to manipulate your chosen metal into the shape you desire.

A helpful tip for beginners: always prioritize safety. Gloves, safety glasses, and a good workspace can make a world of difference. The benefits of metalworking are plenty, from the sense of achievement you get when you create something from scratch, to the practical skills you gain, and not to mention, the cool, metallic art pieces that could make your home look like a modern art gallery!

Origami

Origami is an amazingly creative way to work with your hands. And it's very simple to get started - all you need is some paper! Origami paper is usually square and often colored on one side, but you can start with any paper cut into a square. Start by learning some basic folds and simple shapes. Browse online for tons of ideas, including video tutorials, to help you learn. Origami can be done anywhere and doesn't require much space, so it's a great hobby to take on the go.

The benefits of origami are many. It can help improve your concentration and hand-eye coordination.

It's a calming activity that can help reduce stress, and it's a creative way to create beautiful pieces of art from a simple piece of paper. Plus, it's a fun skill to share with friends and family.

Pottery

Ever wanted to get your hands dirty and get really creative? Then, pottery might just be your new best friend!" From kids to grown-ups, anyone can jump into this earthy hobby. No prerequisites are required, except a willingness to get a little muddy and a lot creative. At first, your clay might seem to have a mind of its own, rebelling against your attempts to shape it.

But with patience and practice, you'll soon be shaping it into pots, vases, or abstract sculptures that even Picasso would nod at approvingly.

Remember, starting slow is key. Master the basic techniques first before you aspire to create a 6-foot vase. The benefits? You'll improve your hand-eye coordination, relieve stress, and hey, you might never have to buy another decorative bowl again!

Calligraphy

Did you know your handwriting could be as elegant as a royal decree with a dash of flair? Welcome to the world of calligraphy!" Anyone can dive into this art, whether you're a scribbler or a sophisticated scribe.

What should you expect? Well, your first few strokes might look more like chicken scratch than exquisite lettering, but don't worry, we all start somewhere. The key is to practice consistently and patiently.

Start with simple alphabets and then progress to words and sentences. And here's a handy tip: keep your work area clean because a blot of ink can swiftly turn a masterpiece into a mess. The benefits are aplenty, from improved concentration to a unique skill that can impress friends or be used in creative projects. Plus, nothing beats the satisfaction of seeing your words transformed into art!

It's also super fun to create unique handwritten cards, invitations, or wall art.

Plus, in a world dominated by digital communication, it's a unique skill that brings back the charm of traditional handwritten letters.

Knitting

Ever wondered how those woolly sheep turn into cozy sweaters? Well, knitting is your ticket to the transformation!" It's an activity that anyone can enjoy - from busy bees looking for a relaxing hobby to grandads wanting to fashion a cute scarf for their grandkids.

It's perfect to do at home, on the train, or anytime you have a few spare minutes to yourself. To begin, you'll need some knitting needles and yarn.

You can find beginner's kits online or at your local craft store. Start by learning the basic stitches: the knit stitch and the purl stitch. From there, you can make a simple project like a scarf or a dishcloth. There are lots of free patterns online.

As you get more experience, you can start making more complex things like hats, blankets, or even sweaters. The benefits of knitting are many. It's a relaxing activity that can help reduce stress. It also improves your hand-eye coordination and fine motor skills. Plus, it's a wonderful feeling to create something warm and cozy with your own hands. And they make super gifts for birthdays and Christmas presents!

Digital Art

Starting digital art as a hobby is a modern way to express your creativity if you love technology. To begin, you'll need a device like a computer or tablet and some digital art software. Programs like Procreate for iPad or Adobe Photoshop for computers are popular choices. A digital stylus can also be helpful for more precise control. Start by experimenting with different brushes, colors, and effects. You can design all sorts from simple drawings to complex landscapes or portraits. Digital art facilitates a lot of experimentation since you can easily undo mistakes and try different options. It can improve your hand-eye coordination and technical skills.

Plus, it's a modern skill that can be useful for many careers in the digital age, from graphic design to animation.

Sewing

Does your closet scream 'last season' louder than a cicada on a hot summer day? Try sewing!" Ideal for both trendsetters aiming to tailor their own style and frugal fellows looking to patch things up, sewing can be a game-changer. Expect to be initially baffled by the mechanics of a sewing machine and the language of patterns, but with a little practice, you'll be threading your way to success. Start with small, straightforward projects - a throw pillow or a tote bag.

Remember to always backstitch at the start and end of your seams for sturdier results.

The perks? Well, besides the skill to whip up an outfit that's so 'you', sewing is a great exercise in patience and precision, and there's no better feeling than wearing something you've made yourself. So, get ready to bid 'off-the-rack' adieu!

It also feels really amazing to create something wearable or useful for your home. Plus, it can save you money on clothes or home decor, and it's a fun way to always have gifts to give for special occasions.

Jewelry Making

Ever looked at a piece of jewelry and thought, 'I could make that!' then jewelry making might just be for you!" This craft is perfect for anyone with a penchant for pretty things, a steady hand, and a heap of creativity. Expect to dive into a treasure chest of beads, wires, and gemstones, with the only limit being your imagination.

Now, don't skimp on the quality of your tools; a good set of pliers can make a world of difference. The benefits of jewelry making are manifold: it's therapeutic, it sparks creativity, and it's a fabulous conversation starter when someone compliments your handcrafted masterpiece. Plus, think of all the bespoke gifts you could make!

In the world of jewelry making, the world really is your oyster (and yes, you can make a necklace out of that too!).

Plus, it can be a relaxing activity that helps reduce stress, and you could even start your own custom jewelry business!

Embroidery

Think you can't handle a needle and thread? Stitch please! Embroidery is for everyone." Whether you're artistically inclined or can't draw a straight line with a ruler, embroidery is a delightful craft for anyone willing to give it a try. Expect a rainbow of thread colors, a variety of patterns, and possibly a pricked finger or two (just kidding, be careful!).

Start with simple designs and work your way up to complex masterpieces. Embroidery has numerous benefits: it's a calming activity that helps with concentration, it boosts creativity, and it results in beautiful, personalized pieces of art you can wear, display, or give as thoughtful gifts.

Start by learning a few basic stitches, such as the running stitch and the backstitch. You can start with easy designs like flowers or letters.. Embroidery is a relaxing activity that can help reduce stress. It improves your hand-eye coordination and attention to detail. Plus, it allows you to create beautiful artwork that can be used to personalize your clothing, make home decor, or give as a unique, handmade gift. Local craft stores often provide classes.

Trust me, nothing quite says 'I care' like a beautifully embroidered handkerchief or a wall hanging that you stitched yourself. Embroidery might just be the hobby you never knew you needed!

Quilting

Ever fallen in love with a beautiful quilt? Or wish you had a gorgeous warm quilt for your bed in the winter. Well, no need to wish anymore! To start quilting as a hobby, you'll need some basic supplies like fabric, a rotary cutter, a cutting mat, a ruler, and a sewing machine. You can find beginner's kits online or at your local craft store. Start by learning how to cut your fabric into squares and sew them together.

Begin with a simple project like a patchwork quilt. There are many free patterns and tutorials online to help guide you. Quilting is a creative activity that can be very relaxing and therapeutic. It also teaches you a valuable skill and there is no feeling like the sense of pride when you finish your first quilt. Plus, it's a wonderful way to create cozy, personalized blankets for your home.

Screen Printing

Ever worn a t-shirt and thought, 'I could do better'? Step right up, screen printing could be your jam!" This creative process is for anyone who's keen on design, art, or just loves the idea of wearing their own creations.

Expect to get a little messy as you smear ink across a stencil to transfer your design onto fabric or paper. One golden rule to remember: always clean your screen straight after printing to keep your designs crisp and clear.

Screen printing is a rewarding hobby, not just because it gives you the power to create custom items, but it also provides a therapeutic and satisfying process to follow. You can create personalized gifts, start a small business, or just enjoy the process as a unique way to express yourself. Be warned, though - once you start screen printing, you might find it hard to stop!

Start with simple designs like words or basic shapes, and you can print them onto t-shirts, tote bags, or posters.

Screen printing is a creative activity that allows you to make custom designs. Plus, it's a practical skill that can be used for making personalized clothing, home decor, or even promotional materials for a business or event.

Glass Blowing

Glass blowing is not just for folks who like the idea of playing with fire! This ancient art form is perfect for those who appreciate the beauty of glass and are unafraid of a challenge. Expect to be in a hot environment and work closely with a flaming furnace, using your breath and various tools to shape molten glass into stunning creations.

Don't forget to dress appropriately - long sleeves and pants can protect you from the heat, and closed-toe shoes are a must. The rewards of glass blowing are substantial. Not only will you gain a sense of accomplishment from creating something beautiful and unique, but the intense focus required can also be a great way to release stress. Plus, who wouldn't want the bragging rights of being able to say, "See that vase? I made it!"

Woodworking

Woodworking - where you can literally turn over a new leaf, or a whole tree if you're ambitious!"

This craft is perfect for those who enjoy working with their hands and have a keen appreciation for the natural beauty of timber. Expect sawdust, lots of it, and the rewarding feeling of transforming a plain piece of wood into a work of art or functional item. Always remember safety first - goggles and gloves are your friends.

Be patient with yourself, mastering the skill takes time but is worth every splinter. Woodworking boosts problem-solving skills, improves focus, and can be a therapeutic way to relax and disconnect from digital distractions. And, of course, nothing beats the satisfaction of answering the question, "Where did you get this beautiful piece?" with a casual, "Oh, I made it."

Woodturning

Woodturning is a form of woodworking where a piece of wood is spun on a lathe and shaped with various tools. To start woodturning as a hobby, you'll need some basic equipment like a lathe, woodturning chisels, and safety gear like goggles and a dust mask.

You can find beginner's kits online or at your local hardware store. I would recommend before you invest in tools, you join a local woodturning class to get hands-on experience.

Start by learning how to safely use your lathe and how to shape the wood with different chisels. Begin with a simple project like a wooden pen or a small bowl.

Woodturning is a unique form of woodworking that allows you to create rounded items that would be difficult to make with regular tools. It's also a therapeutic activity that can help reduce stress. Plus, it's a satisfying skill to master and can result in beautiful, functional items you can use yourself or give as gifts.

Car Restoration

Car restoration is ideal for those who have a passion for automobiles and the patience of a saint. Expect grease-stained hands, hours spent hunting for the perfect replacement parts, and the sweet victory of an engine roaring to life after a successful repair.

Handy tip: start with a simple project car and gradually work your way up to more complex models. The benefits of car restoration are manifold. It provides an incredible sense of achievement, keeps your problem-solving skills sharp, and allows you to tangibly see the fruits of your labor. Plus, the pride you feel when you cruise around in a car that you've restored yourself? Priceless!

Model Building

Model building is where your living room can host the Eiffel Tower, the Statue of Liberty, and a Tyrannosaurus Rex, all on the same coffee table! This hobby is perfect for those with a keen eye for detail and an appreciation for patience.

Expect small parts, plenty of concentration, and the joy of seeing miniature versions of real-life or fantasy entities take shape right in front of you.

Invest in a good set of tweezers and remember, it's not a race - take your time. The benefits are plentiful; not only does model building enhance your focus and dexterity, it also feeds your creativity and provides a fantastic feeling of accomplishment when you've finished.

And let's face it, there's something quite fun about having a scale model of a famous landmark or a prehistoric beast right there on your bookshelf!

Photography & film

Photography

Starting photography as a hobby is easier than you might think. All you need is a camera, and it doesn't have to be an expensive one. Even a smartphone can take great photos these days. Start by taking photos of things you like or find interesting. This could be people, landscapes, animals, or anything else that catches your eye. Look for online tutorials to learn about different techniques, like how to use lighting, how to compose a shot, and how to edit your photos. Practice regularly and experiment with different styles to see what you enjoy most. Photography can also be really relaxing.

Plus, you'll end up with beautiful photos that capture your unique view of the world.

Films

Filming making is an incredible hobby that you can end up at international film festivals with, and to begin you don't even need fancy equipment. A smartphone with a good camera and simple editing software can be enough. Start by experimenting with short videos. Experiment with a day in your life to a small story idea you have. As you film, consider elements like lighting, shot composition, and storytelling. You can find lots of free lessons online that can teach you the basics of filmmaking. Once you've filmed your footage, you can use editing software to put it all together.

Apps like iMovie (for Apple devices) or FilmoraGo (for Android) can be great starting points. The benefits of filmmaking as a hobby are numerous. It can help you express your creativity, tell stories in a unique way, and develop a new appreciation for the movies and TV shows you love. Plus, it's a lot of fun and can lead to a fulfilling pastime or even a future career.

Short films

"Shorts" in film refer to short films, which are films that are significantly shorter than a typical full-length feature film. There isn't a set length for what constitutes a short film, but generally, they are under 40 minutes in length, including all credits. Some short films are even just a few minutes long.

Short films are a popular format for filmmakers to explore an idea, tell a compact story, or showcase their filmmaking skills. They often focus on a single incident or character and aim to create a strong impression within a short span of time.

Many filmmakers start their careers making short films, which can be a stepping stone to feature-length films. Short films are also a popular format in film festivals and online platforms where they can be shared and viewed easily. If you make a short film you can also submit it to film festivals around the world!

Documentaries

Making a documentary can be life changing experience. To start, you need to pick a topic that you're passionate about. It could be a local event, an interesting person, a historical event, or even a personal interest or hobby.

Next, you need to do your research. This can take a lot of research. Then, plan your film. Think about the story you want to tell and how you want to tell it. You might need to conduct interviews, film events, or collect archival footage.

You can film using a DSLR camera or even a smartphone. Once you've collected your footage, you can use editing software to put it all together.

There are free editing software options available.

Making a documentary can help you learning more about a topic you're interested in, develop new skills, and have the chance to tell important stories that can even end up on the big screen! Plus, it's a creative outlet that allows you to share your perspective with others. You can enter your finished documentary in local and international film festivals too.

Writing

Publish a memoir

Writing and self-publishing a memoir is a journey of self-discovery and storytelling. Here are a few tips to get you started:

Find Your Story

Everyone has a unique story to tell. Start by jotting down memories, experiences, and people that have had a major impact on your life. Remember, a memoir is not an autobiography. You don't need to cover your whole life, just a particular aspect or period that you find meaningful and think others might too.

Outline Your Book

When you have an outline of what your memoir will cover, create an outline. This will serve as your roadmap while writing. It doesn't have to be detailed; just list the main events or points you want to cover in each chapter.

Start Writing

Start filling in your outline with detailed descriptions, dialogues, thoughts, and emotions. Don't worry about making it perfect in the first draft; just get your story down. Write regularly, make it a habit.

Edit and Revise

After you've written your first draft, take some time to revise and edit. Look for any inconsistencies, grammatical errors, and areas where you can improve clarity or add more detail. Get feedback from trusted friends or hire a professional editor.

Prepare for Publication

While your manuscript is being edited, start thinking about the other elements of your book. You'll need a captivating title and an engaging book cover. You can hire a designer to make the cover or use free online design tools if you're comfortable doing it yourself.

Self-Publishing

When you're happy with your manuscript, it's time to publish. There are several online platforms for self-publishing. They all have step-by-step guides to upload your book and set a price. Remember, they will take a small percentage of your sales.

Marketing Your Memoir

Now that your memoir is published, you need to let people know about it. Share the news on social media, your blog, or website. Contact local bookstores, libraries, or book clubs. Consider creating a catchy book description and encourage readers to leave reviews.

Writing and self-publishing a memoir can be a rewarding experience, allowing you to share your life's significant moments with others while leaving a tangible piece of your legacy. Go slowly, be patient with yourself, and enjoy the process.

Write a children's picture book

Creating and self-publishing a children's picture book can be a fun and rewarding project. Here's a simple step-by-step guide:

Find Your Story

Start by brainstorming ideas for your story. Children's picture books are usually short, simple, and often deliver a moral or message.

They're typically designed for children aged 3-8 years old.

Write the Story

Once you have your idea, start writing. Remember to keep the language simple and the story engaging. Children's picture books usually have less than 1,000 words and the story is often told more through the pictures than the text.

Plan Your Illustrations

Picture books are all about visuals. Start planning what kind of images you'd like to accompany your story. You can sketch them out or write descriptions of what you envision.

Hire an Illustrator

Unless you're an artist yourself, you might want to hire a professional illustrator. You can find illustrators on websites like Fiverr, Upwork, or through children's book illustrators' societies. Remember, the style of the illustrations should match the tone of your story.

Create a Book Dummy

A book dummy is a mock-up of your book. It helps you plan how your text and illustrations will fit together on each page.

You can create a simple book dummy by folding pieces of paper in half to represent pages and sketching out where the text and pictures will go.

Edit and Proofread

Check for any spelling or grammar errors. Read your story out loud - this is a great way to make sure it flows well. Consider getting feedback from others, especially children!

Prepare for Publication

Now it's time to put your book together. Choose a size for your book and export a final version of your manuscript with the illustrations, usually into a PDF.

Self-Publishing

There are many online platforms for self-publishing, like KDP or Blurb. These platforms have step-by-step guides to help you upload your book, set a price, and choose where you want to sell it.

Marketing Your Book

Spread the word about your book. Share your book with your family, tell your friends, put your book cover on social media, and at local events. Consider sending copies to bloggers, reviewers, and influencers who can help promote your book.

Remember, creating a children's picture book is a big project, but it's also a lot of fun.

Enjoy the process. You're creating something that can spark a child's imagination and love for reading!

Write a poetry book

Writing your first poetry book is a creative journey that starts with you and your thoughts. I'd recommend that you begin by writing individual poems. Don't worry about how they fit together just yet - focus on expressing your feelings and experiences. Write regularly and try different styles to find your unique voice.

Once you have a collection of poems, think about how you might organise them into a book. Look for common themes or ideas that can help organize your book.

You might choose to edit your poems or write new ones to fill in any gaps. When you're happy with your collection, you can think about self-publishing or submitting your book to a publisher. The benefits of writing a poetry book are many. It can help you express yourself, deal with emotions, and see the world in new ways. Plus, you'll have a beautiful collection of your work that you can share with others.

Write a letter to your local newspaper

If you feel strongly about something, you can share your opinions, bring attention to a cause, or highlight something positive happening in your community, by writing a letter to your local newspaper.

To start, you need to write a clear and concise letter. Begin by stating your purpose for writing. If you're responding to an article, mention the title and date of the article. Then, share your thoughts or information. Keep your points focused and support your views with facts or personal experiences. Include your name, address, and a phone number at the end - newspapers need this to verify your letter, but they will only publish your name and city. Once your letter is written, you can usually email it to the newspaper's letters section (you can find this email address on their website). This could be an exciting step to engage with your community, influence public opinion, and potentially affect change on issues you care about. Plus, it feels great to see your name in print!

Write a press release to help a local business

Writing a press release for a local business is an effective way to get the word out about what they're doing. Let's get started!

Choose a Business

First, you need to choose which local business you'd like to write about. Maybe it's a business that you love or one that you feel is making a positive impact in your community. You could also choose a business that has a special event coming up soon, or a new product/service they'd like to promote.

Gather Information

Once you've chosen a business, you need to gather information. This might include talking to the business owner or employees, visiting the business yourself, or doing some online research. Research how the business services its customers, what makes it unique, and what the news is that you'll be sharing in the press release.

Write the Headline

Your press release needs a catchy headline. This headline will ideally sum up the news you're sharing and grab people's attention.

Write the Body

The body of the press release provides more details about the news. This might include quotes from the business owner, more information about the business, and details about the event, product, or service you're promoting.

Contact Information

Include contact information at the end of the press release. This should be the name, phone number, and email address of the person who can answer any questions about the press release.

Review and Edit

Make sure to review your press release for any errors and to make sure it reads well. Ask a friend to look over it as well.

Distribute the Press Release

Now you can send your press release to the local business and give them some suggestions about local newspapers, radio stations, and online news sites they could send it too. They can put it on social media or on the business's website.

Remember, make your press release as interesting and human focused as you can, and make sure to focus on the news that you're sharing. Good luck!

Write a short story

A short story is a small work of fiction, similar to a novel but much shorter and focuses on a single incident. You need just a pen and paper or a computer to get started.

This form teaches you to write concisely and make every word count. Keep your story focused and try to create a big impact with a few words.

Start a blog

A blog is a website where you can write about your thoughts, experiences, or interests. You can share things like stories, tips, recipes, reviews, or any other type of content you enjoy. To start a blog, you'll first need to choose a topic or theme that you're passionate about. Then, you can use a blogging platform to create your blog. The popular platforms are very user-friendly and many of them offer free options.

You'll then need to write your first post and publish it. Start with a short introduction about yourself and what your blog will be about. The benefits of blogging are many. You can express yourself and share your ideas with the world. Plus, if your blog gains a large audience, it might earn you money through things like advertising or sponsored posts.

Write a screenplay

Screenplays are used for movies and TV shows. A screenplay includes the dialogue that characters will say, as well as descriptions of the scenes and actions. To write a screenplay, you first need a story idea.

Then, create an outline of your story, including the main events and the flow of the plot. You can then start writing the screenplay itself, using a specific format that includes things like scene headings, character names, and dialogue. You can find templates and guides for this format online. Start with a short screenplay for a short film. Screenwriting can really improve your writing skills, especially in terms of dialogue and visual storytelling. Plus, if your screenplay is good, it could potentially be made into a film or TV show.

Start a journal

Journaling is a really popular way to express your thoughts and feelings, often on a daily basis.

You just need a notebook or a computer. Journaling can improve self-awareness and emotional wellbeing. There are no rules in journal writing, just be honest with yourself.

Songwriting

Writing a song involves creating lyrics and often music to convey a certain emotion or story. You'll need a pen and paper and an instrument. You can find programs online to help you write songs also. Songwriting can help you express emotions and tell stories in a unique way. Listen to lots of music and don't be afraid to rewrite and revise your songs.

To start writing songs, you can begin by brainstorming ideas or emotions you want to express.

Then, you can choose a genre or style of music that suits your preferences or the message you want to convey. There are various genres to explore, such as pop, rock, country, hip-hop, or folk. You can start by writing the lyrics first, or by creating the music first, it's up to you!

When writing, you can experiment with chord progressions, melodies, and lyrics that fit the genre you've chosen. Songwriting allows you to express yourself creatively, share your thoughts and emotions, and connect with others on a deep level. Writing songs can be a therapeutic outlet and a way to communicate your experiences and stories. It could even lead to a career in music if you choose to pursue it further.

Vacation adventures

Who says you need to be an astronaut to explore new worlds? You just need a plane ticket! Travelling abroad is for anyone with a sense of adventure, whether you're young, old, solo, or with family. Expect to meet different cultures, try new foods, learn a few phrases in another language, and see sights that postcards can't do justice. You'll broaden your horizons, experience diverse ways of life, and collect unforgettable memories. Plus, you'll have the best stories at your next social gathering. So pack your bags and let's hit the road, or rather, the sky! Here are some ideas to get you started.

USA

Exploring Alaska's Natural Wonders (Alaska)

Alaska is perfect for nature lovers. From glacier hiking in Kenai Fjords National Park to watching the Northern Lights, this state is full of awe-inspiring sights. Summer, specifically June through August, is the best time to visit, as the weather is warmest and the days are long. This is the high season, so booking in advance is recommended. Don't forget to pack layers and sturdy footwear for your outdoor adventures!

Jazz, Jambalaya and Joy in New Orleans (Louisiana)

New Orleans is full of amazing cultures, music, and mouth-watering cuisine.

Visit during Mardi Gras (usually in February) for an unforgettable experience, or in April for the world-famous New Orleans Jazz & Heritage Festival. While there, take a historic riverboat cruise on the Mississippi, and explore the unique architecture of the French Quarter. Tip: Be sure to try the beignets at Cafe du Monde!

Road Tripping Route 66 (Illinois to California)

Experience the quintessential American journey from Chicago to Santa Monica along historic Route 66. You'll experience a diverse array of landscapes and quirky roadside attractions. Spring and Fall are the best times to go, as you'll avoid the summer heat and winter snow.

Tip: Make sure to plan your stops, but also allow for some spontaneity!

Discovering the National Parks of Utah (Utah)

Known as the 'Mighty 5', Utah's national parks (Canyonlands, Bryce Canyon, Arches, Capitol Reef and Zion) offer stunning landscapes of rock formations and canyons. Spring (April-May) and Fall (September-October) offer comfortable temperatures for hiking. Remember to pack plenty of water, wear sun protection, and respect the natural environment.

Island Hopping in Hawaii (Hawaii)

With its beautiful beaches, active volcanoes, and lush rainforests, Hawaii is a tropical paradise. Each island has its unique charm, from the dramatic cliffs of Kauai to the iconic surf of Oahu. The best time to visit is generally April-May and September-October. This is when the weather is very nice and the tourist crowds are smaller. Tip: Don't forget to attend a traditional luau for a taste of Hawaiian culture!

Cruising the Florida Keys (Florida)

The Florida Keys are a series of tropical islands in the USA. They stretch about 120 miles from the south of the U.S. state of Florida.

Enjoy the laid-back beach life, explore the coral reefs, or try your hand at fishing in the sport fishing capital of the world. I would recommend to visit between March and May, when temperatures are comfortable and accommodation prices are reasonable. Don't forget to enjoy a slice of key lime pie!

Skiing in Aspen (Colorado)

If you love winter sports, Aspen is a must-visit. This Rocky Mountain ski resort town offers world-class skiing and snowboarding, along with fine dining and high-end shopping. The ski season runs from late November to early April. Remember to book your accommodations and lift tickets in advance as this popular destination can get busy.

Wine Tasting in Napa Valley (California)

Napa Valley is famous for its incredible vineyards. Visit during the fall to see the grape leaves changing color and to enjoy the grape harvest, or in the spring for beautiful weather and fewer crowds. Don't miss a hot air balloon ride for a stunning view of the valley. Tip: Consider booking a wine tour, so you don't have to worry about driving after tasting!

Exploring the Grand Canyon (Arizona)

The Grand Canyon is one of the Seven Natural Wonders of the World.

It offers breathtaking views that photos can't do justice. Hike, take a helicopter tour, or just enjoy the view. Spring (March-May) and fall (September-November) offer milder weather. Remember to wear comfortable shoes and carry plenty of water if you plan to hike.

Touring the Historic Charleston (South Carolina)

Known for its well-preserved architecture, rich history, distinguished restaurants, and mannerly people, Charleston has been named the No. 1 U.S. city by Travel + Leisure's World's Best Awards numerous times.

I would recommend to visit in the spring when temperatures are mild, gardens are in bloom, and the festival season is in full swing. Don't miss a visit to the historic Charleston City Market to pick up a sweetgrass basket or other local handcrafts.

Experiencing New York City (New York)

New York offers something for everyone. From Broadway shows and iconic landmarks like the Statue of Liberty and Central Park, to a diverse food scene, there's no shortage of things to do. While NYC can be visited any time of the year, the city is particularly magical during the holiday season with festive lights and decorations.

Remember to book tickets in advance for popular attractions!

Camping in Yellowstone National Park (Wyoming, Montana, Idaho)

As America's first national park, Yellowstone is renowned for its geysers, hot springs, and diverse wildlife. Avoid the summer crowds and visit in the spring and fall, but be aware that parts of the park may be closed due to snow. Tip: Pack a good pair of binoculars for wildlife viewing!

Exploring the Music Scene in Nashville (Tennessee)

Known as Music City, Nashville is a must-visit for country music fans.

Visit during June for the CMA Music Festival, or anytime of the year to catch live performances at the Grand Ole Opry and explore the Country Music Hall of Fame. Don't forget to indulge in the city's famous hot chicken!

Driving the Pacific Coast Highway (California)

This epic road trip offers stunning coastal views, charming seaside towns, and notable landmarks like the Bixby Bridge and Hearst Castle. The best time for this trip is during the spring or fall to avoid summer traffic and winter road closures. Relax and enjoy the journey – there are plenty of scenic pullouts for photo ops!

Each of these bucket list holidays offers a unique slice of America, allowing you to explore the diverse natural beauty, rich history, and vibrant cultures found across the country.

UK

Exploring the Historic Edinburgh (Edinburgh, Scotland)

The Scottish capital is a city steeped in history and culture. Visit the iconic Edinburgh Castle, walk the Royal Mile, and explore the Old and New Towns, both of which are UNESCO World Heritage Sites. I would recommend to visit during the summer, especially in August when the world-famous Edinburgh Festival Fringe takes place. Tip: Don't miss a hike up Arthur's Seat for panoramic views of the city!

Touring the English Countryside in the Cotswolds (Gloucestershire and Oxfordshire, England)

The Cotswolds is known for its picturesque villages, rolling hills, and historic manors. It's a perfect place for a relaxing countryside holiday. Spring (May-June) is a beautiful time to visit when the wildflowers are in bloom. Tip: Be sure to try a traditional cream tea in a cosy village tearoom!

Experiencing the Cultural Hub of London (Greater London, England)

From historic sites like the Tower of London and Buckingham Palace, to cultural attractions like the British Museum and the West End theatres, London is an amazing city for all ages. London can be visited year-round, but the warmer months of May to September offer the best weather for sightseeing. Remember to use the extensive public transportation system, which includes the London Underground, buses, and even river ferries.

Walking the Ancient Roman Baths in Bath (Somerset, England)

Bath is a UNESCO World Heritage Site, known for its well-preserved Roman Baths, stunning Georgian architecture, and the iconic Royal Crescent. The city is beautiful year-round, but visiting in the spring or fall allows you to avoid the summer crowds. Tip: Don't miss a visit to the Thermae Bath Spa, where you can soak in the natural thermal waters!

Exploring the Rugged Beauty of the Lake District (Cumbria, England)

The Lake District is famous for its stunning lakes, mountains, and historic literary associations.

It's a paradise for walkers, hikers, and lovers of the great outdoors. Summer (June-August) provides the best weather, but it's also the busiest time, so booking accommodations in advance is recommended.

Ireland

Discovering the Capital City of Dublin (County Dublin)

As Ireland's capital, Dublin is a vibrant city known for its historic landmarks, literary heritage, and the famous Guinness Brewery. Visit the Book of Kells at Trinity College, explore Temple Bar, or explore the historic Dublin Castle.

I would recommend visiting Dublin during the spring and summer months (May to September) when the weather is pleasant. Tip: Find a local pub and participate in a traditional Irish music session!

Exploring the Breathtaking Cliffs of Moher (County Clare)

These majestic sea cliffs are one of Ireland's most visited natural attractions. Walking along the cliff tops, you'll be treated to panoramic views of the Atlantic Ocean and the Aran Islands. The cliffs are beautiful year-round, but the weather tends to be most agreeable in the summer (June-August). Wear a wrap jacket and be prepared for sudden weather changes.

Driving the Ring of Kerry (County Kerry)

The Ring of Kerry takes you through some of Ireland's most spectacular landscapes, including mountains, beaches, and lakes. Along the way, you'll find charming villages, ancient ruins, and plenty of spots for a picnic. The best time for this trip is during the summer, to enjoy some nice weather. Tip: Drive counter-clockwise to go with the tour bus flow and enjoy a less rushed experience.

Touring the Ancient Sites of Boyne Valley (County Meath)

Boyne Valley is a World Heritage Site and is the location of ancient burial grounds, including the famous Newgrange, Knowth, and Dowth. The valley is also rich in medieval history, with the Hill of Tara and Trim Castle to explore. Visit in the summer when the days are longer. Tip: Plan to visit during the Winter Solstice, when a lottery winner gets to witness the sunrise light up the passage tomb at Newgrange.

Experiencing the Wild Atlantic Way (West Coast of Ireland)

This long-distance touring route spans nine counties and offers breathtaking coastal scenery, charming seaside towns, and diverse cultural experiences.

Highlights include the Dingle Peninsula in County Kerry, the Cliffs of Moher (County Clare), and Connemara in County Galway. The best time to drive the Wild Atlantic Way is from late spring to early fall. Tip: Take your time and make plenty of stops to truly appreciate the beauty and charm of this route.

Europe

Exploring the Romantic City of Paris (France)

Paris is famous the Eiffel Tower, Louvre Museum, and Notre-Dame Cathedral. Its food, fashion, and culture make it a must-visit. Visit during the spring (April-June) when the weather is mild. Remember to try the local cuisine, and don't forget to say "bonjour" when entering shops – it's customary!

Touring the Historic Rome (Italy)

With its rich history and vibrant culture, Rome is a treasure trove of ancient sites including the Colosseum, Roman Forum, and the Pantheon.

Don't miss Vatican City and its magnificent St. Peter's Basilica. The best time to visit Rome is from April to June and late September to October when the weather is warm and comfortable. Tip: Be prepared for the 'coperto' – a small charge added to your bill in most Italian restaurants.

Experiencing the Unique Istanbul (Turkey)

Straddling Europe and Asia, Istanbul offers a blend of cultures, a rich history, and incredible architecture, including the Blue Mosque and Hagia Sophia. The bustling Grand Bazaar is a shopper's paradise.

Visit during the spring or fall when to maximize your chances of pleasant weather. You will need to dress modestly if you plan to visit religious sites.

Exploring the Vibrant Barcelona (Spain)

Barcelona is a city known for its unique architecture, particularly the works of Antoni Gaudí, including the famous Sagrada Familia. Enjoy the city's rich art scene, delicious tapas, and beautiful beaches. Visit from May to June when temperatures are just right. Tip: Purchase tickets online in advance for major attractions to skip the queues.

Cruising the Greek Islands (Greece)

The Greek Islands offer stunning landscapes, beautiful beaches, and rich history. Each island is unique, from the sunset views in Santorini to the vibrant nightlife in Mykonos. Visit during the shoulder seasons of spring (April to early-June) and fall (September and October) when the weather is pleasant and there are fewer tourists. Tip: Keep in mind that many businesses on the islands close during the off-season, from late October to April.

Canada

Witnessing the Natural Wonder of Niagara Falls (Ontario)

Niagara Falls is actually the name for three waterfalls on the border between Canada and the USA. Visit the observation decks or take a boat tour for a close-up view. Visit during the summer months (June-August) when all the attractions are open. Tip: Don't forget your raincoat or poncho, as you'll get wet from the mist!

Exploring the Vibrant City of Toronto (Ontario)

As Canada's largest city, Toronto offers a myriad of attractions, from the iconic CN Tower to the bustling St. Lawrence Market.

The city has an amazing food scene. Visit during the spring (April-June) or fall (September-November) when the weather is comfortable. Remember to use the city's excellent public transportation system to get around.

Touring the Historic Quebec City (Quebec)

Quebec City's historic district, a UNESCO World Heritage site, has lots of narrow cobblestone streets and houses from the 17th and 18th-centuries. Visit during the winter for the annual Winter Carnival, or in the summer for the city's music festival. Tip: Brush up on your French, as Quebec is a predominantly French-speaking province.

Experiencing the Beauty of Banff National Park (Alberta)

Nestled in the Canadian Rockies, Banff National Park offers stunning mountain landscapes, turquoise glacial lakes, and abundant wildlife. Activities include hiking, skiing, and bird-watching. Visit during the summer months (June-August) or during ski season (December-March). Remember to pack for variable weather as mountain weather can be unpredictable.

Exploring the Coastal Beauty of Vancouver (British Columbia)

Vancouver is known for its beautiful coastline, towering mountains, and vibrant city life.

Visit Stanley Park, Granville Island, or take a day trip to nearby Whistler. Visit during the summer (June-August) when the weather is nice. Tip: Consider using the city's bike-sharing program.

Australia & NZ

Exploring the Natural Beauty of Milford Sound (South Island, New Zealand)

Located within Fiordland National Park, Milford Sound offers stunning fiords, dramatic cliffs, and cascading waterfalls. Cruise the sound or take a kayak trip for a closer look. Visit during the summer (December-February) when the weather is typically milder. Tip: Be prepared for wet weather – Milford Sound is one of the rainiest inhabited places in New Zealand, but the rain makes the waterfalls even more spectacular!

Experiencing the Cosmopolitan Sydney (New South Wales, Australia)

Sydney has many iconic landmarks like the Harbour Bridge and Sydney Opera House. Enjoy the vibrant arts scene, diverse cuisine, and beautiful beaches like Bondi and Manly. Visit in spring (September-November) or autumn (March-May) when the weather is pleasant. Tip: Don't miss a ferry ride across the harbour for stunning city views.

Exploring the Great Barrier Reef (Queensland, Australia)

The Great Barrier Reef is the world's largest coral reef system, home to a rich diversity of marine life. You can snorkel, dive, or take a boat tour to explore this natural wonder.

Visit during the Australian winter (June-August) when the weather is mild and the water is clear. Remember to follow all guidelines to help protect the reef!

Discovering the Wildlife on Kangaroo Island (South Australia, Australia)

Kangaroo Island is teeming with native Australian wildlife, including kangaroos, koalas, and sea lions. It also offers beautiful landscapes, from pristine beaches to national parks. Visit during the Australian summer (December-February) when the weather is warm. Tip: Rent a car to explore the island at your own pace.

Visiting the Cultural Capital Melbourne (Victoria, Australia)

Melbourne is known for its vibrant arts scene, multicultural food, and sports culture. Explore the laneways, visit the museums, and enjoy a game of Aussie Rules Football or cricket. Visit during the autumn (March-May) when the weather is mild and the city hosts several significant events. Remember to check out the coffee culture - Melbourne is famous for its coffee!

South America

Exploring the Lost City of Machu Picchu (Peru)

Nestled in the Andean mountains, the ancient Incan city of Machu Picchu is one of South America's most iconic landmarks. Visit during the dry season, from May to September. Remember to acclimate to the altitude in Cusco before heading to Machu Picchu. Tip: Book your tickets well in advance, especially to hike the Inca Trail.

Cruising the Amazon River (Brazil, Peru, Ecuador)

The Amazon Rainforest is the largest tropical rainforest in the world.

And a cruise on the Amazon River is a unique way to explore it. See exotic wildlife, meet indigenous communities, and immerse yourself in the lush landscape. Visit during the dry season (June to November) when wildlife viewing is optimal. Remember to pack insect repellent and lightweight, long-sleeved clothing.

Visiting the Vibrant City of Buenos Aires (Argentina)

Buenos Aires, aka the "Paris of South America" offers a rich cultural experience, from tango dancing and soccer games to world-class dining.

Visit during the fall (March-May) or spring (September-November) when the weather is pleasant. Don't forget to try the country's famous steak and Malbec wine.

Touring the Salar de Uyuni (Bolivia)

Salar de Uyuni is the world's largest salt flat, and offers a surreal, otherworldly landscape that's a photographer's dream. Visit during the rainy season (December-April) when a thin layer of water transforms the flats into a giant mirror. Tip: Make sure you choose a reputable tour operator for your trip to ensure safety and responsible travel practices.

Hiking the Torres del Paine National Park (Chile)

This park is a hiker's paradise, with its striking mountain peaks, bright blue glaciers, and diverse wildlife. Visit during the summer (December-March) when all the trails are open. Tip: Be prepared for changeable weather and pack accordingly.

Dance classes

If you've been known to clear a dance floor with your two left feet, worry not! There's a dance class out there ready to turn your awkward shuffle into a confident strut. Here are 10 types you could try:

Ballet

This classical dance form requires grace, precision, and discipline. Expect to start with the basic positions and barre exercises. To get started, you'll need a pair of ballet shoes and comfortable clothing. Ballet improves flexibility, strength, and posture.

Hip-Hop

This energetic style often involves freestyle movement and high energy routines. Expect to learn various moves and combinations to upbeat music. Wear comfortable clothing and sneakers. Hip-hop can be a great cardio workout and a way to express yourself.

Salsa

This Latin dance is all about rhythm and flair. In salsa classes, you'll learn how to move with a partner to fast-paced music. Wear shoes that allow for easy turning. Salsa is fun, social, and a good way to improve coordination.

Ballroom Dancing

Here you'll learn dances like the waltz, tango, and foxtrot. Expect to work with a partner and learn specific step patterns. Formal shoes are recommended. Ballroom dancing is great for posture, and it's also quite the social event!

Belly Dancing

This Middle Eastern dance involves a lot of torso articulation. You'll learn to isolate different parts of your body to create smooth movements. Comfortable clothing that allows for movement is best. Belly dancing can improve core strength and flexibility.

Zumba

This is a dance fitness program that incorporates Latin rhythms with cardiovascular exercise. Expect an energetic, high-intensity class. Wear workout attire and comfortable shoes. Zumba is great for weight loss and overall fitness.

Tap Dancing

This dance style uses the sound of tap shoes hitting the floor as a type of percussion. You'll learn different rhythms and routines. Tap shoes are necessary for this class. Tap dance is excellent for improving rhythm and coordination.

Jazz

Jazz often involves unique moves, big leaps, and quick turns. Expect an energetic class set to a variety of music styles. Jazz shoes or dance sneakers are recommended. Jazz dance can improve flexibility, strength, and rhythm.

Pole Dancing

This form of performance art involves dancing and acrobatics using a vertical pole. Expect to learn spins, climbs, and inverts. Wear shorts and a tank top. Pole dance is a full-body workout that improves strength, flexibility, and confidence.

Line Dancing

This choreographed dance involves a repeated sequence of steps, usually performed in a group. Expect to learn a series of dances to country music. Comfortable clothing and shoes are recommended. Line dancing is a fun, social way to keep fit.

So, put on your dancing shoes, find the beat, and let the rhythm move you - it's time to dance!

Music

Can playing a musical instrument make you smarter? Well, at least that's what we musicians like to believe! Jokes aside, learning to play an instrument can be a wonderful journey of self-expression, discipline, and joy. Here are 10 musical instruments that you could start with.

Learn to play an instrument
Guitar

Ever wanted to be the life of a party without having to tell a single joke? Just strum a guitar! Learning to play the guitar is for everyone who's ever hummed a tune, whether you're seven or seventy. Expect your fingertips to toughen up, your ear for music to become more attuned, and your understanding of rhythm to deepen.

Keep your guitar in a place where you can easily see and reach for it, this way, practicing will become part of your daily routine. The benefits are sweet: besides impressing your friends, playing guitar can be a great stress reliever and a creative outlet. Plus, who knows?

With enough practice, you might just end up writing the next hit song, right there in your living room!

Piano

This classic instrument requires both hands working together yet doing different things. You'll start with simple scales and basic songs. A keyboard or piano and a beginner's guide are essential. You can expect some sore fingers at first and perhaps a few off-key notes, but don't worry – even Beethoven started somewhere!

Violin

This string instrument is known for its beautiful, soulful sound.

Expect to learn how to hold the violin and bow, and play basic notes. A violin, bow, and rosin are your starting tools. Playing the violin can enhance posture and concentration.

Drums

This rhythmic instrument sets the beat for any music. Expect to learn basic beats and rhythm patterns. A drum kit and a pair of drumsticks are needed. Drumming can be a great stress reliever and improves coordination.

Flute

This woodwind instrument is lightweight and portable.

You'll start with learning how to blow correctly and finger simple notes. A flute and a beginner's book are essential. Playing the flute can enhance lung capacity and discipline.

Saxophone

This instrument is known for its rich, expressive tones. Expect to learn breath control and finger positioning. A saxophone, reeds, and a beginner's guide can get you started. Playing the saxophone can improve breathing and cognitive abilities, and what jazz band doesn't need a sax player?

Clarinet

This woodwind instrument is popular in jazz and classical pieces. You'll start with learning how to assemble the instrument and play basic notes. A clarinet, reeds, and a beginner's book are needed. Playing the clarinet can improve lung function and discipline.

Ukulele

This small string instrument is relatively easy to learn. You'll start with simple chords and strumming patterns. A ukulele and a beginner's guide can get you started. Playing the ukulele can be a fun way to improve fine motor skills and boost mood.

Harmonica

This pocket-sized instrument is great for blues and folk music. Expect to learn breath control and simple tunes. A harmonica and a beginner's guide are essential. Playing the harmonica can enhance lung capacity and hand-eye coordination.

Cello

This string instrument is known for its deep, warm sound. You'll start with holding the cello and bow correctly and playing open strings. A cello, bow, and rosin are your starting tools. Playing the cello can improve posture and concentration.

So, choose your instrument, tune up, and start making some noise – it's time to play!

Start singing lessons

Ready to become the next big singing sensation? Or maybe just impress your shower tiles with some new high notes? Whatever your motivation, taking singing lessons could be your golden ticket. Perfect for beginners to experienced crooners, singing lessons are designed to cater to all levels.

In weekly singing lessons, you'll learn the basics like pitch, tone, and rhythm. For the more advanced, expect to delve into different vocal styles, techniques, and even songwriting. Maybe one day you could release your own album! The most important tip? Don't be shy!

Everyone starts somewhere, and remember that your voice is unique. It's a fun way to improve confidence, self-expression, and even your lung capacity and posture. Plus, it's a fantastic way to relieve stress. So go ahead, warm up those vocal cords and get ready to serenade the world, one note at a time!

Become a rockstar

Alright superstar, ready to start a band and take over the world one power chord at a time? Well, you're in for a thrilling, occasionally chaotic, but always rewarding ride!

Starting a rock band begins with finding your band members.

You'll need a mix of aspiring musicians who love music too - think drummer, bassist, guitarist, and of course, the lead vocalist. But remember, a rock band isn't just about making great music; it's about camaraderie, so choose people you vibe with. Once your band is formed, the fun (and real work) starts. Expect long hours of practice, learning to play together, and creating your unique sound. Begin with cover songs to hone your skills before branching out into original compositions.

And don't be disheartened by initial hiccups; it's all part of the process.

A few tips for rookies: Practice makes perfect, so jam together often. Listen to a lot of music to draw inspiration. Be open to constructive criticism.

Network, perform at local gigs, and get your name out there.

Being in a rock band has its perks. It's a fantastic outlet for creativity and expression. It'll help improve your musical skills, and the camaraderie and shared experiences with your bandmates are priceless. Plus, there's nothing quite like the adrenaline rush of performing live on stage! And there are no age limits to becoming a rockstar. So, grab your leather jacket, strap on that electric guitar, and get ready to rock 'n roll. Your fans await!

Join an orchestra

So, you're dreaming of diving into the deep end of the musical pool, are you?

Well, joining an orchestra is like being a fish in a symphonic sea, and it's quite a journey! Joining an orchestra usually requires a certain level of proficiency with your instrument, so beginners may want to notch up some private lessons first. For intermediate or advanced players, an audition is typically the next step to demonstrate your skills. Expect to play a piece of your choice and possibly some sight-reading.

A few tips for the orchestral greenhorns: Practice is key, and so is punctuality - showing up late for rehearsal is a big no-no. Be open to feedback and take it in stride, as it will only make you a better musician.

Get to know your fellow orchestra members; they can offer great advice and make the experience more enjoyable. Besides improving your musical skills, it provides a fantastic social network of like-minded individuals. There's also the thrill of performing in front of an audience and the opportunity to play a diverse range of music. So, tune up your instrument, dust off that tuxedo, and get ready to create some harmonious magic. Your standing ovation is just around the corner!

Join a choir

Ready to harmonize with a group of like minded friends? Welcome to the uplifting world of choir singing!

Joining a choir is an experience that's open to singers of all levels. From novices who can barely hold a tune to seasoned vocalists, there's a choir out there for everyone. Typically, you'll need to audition, demonstrating your ability to match pitch and harmonize with others. But don't worry, most choir directors are more interested in your enthusiasm than a pitch-perfect performance.

As for what to expect, picture weekly rehearsals where you'll learn to blend your voice with others, master a wide variety of songs, and occasionally break into spontaneous renditions of 'Bohemian Rhapsody'. A tip for choir newbies: Stay hydrated, it keeps those vocal cords happy.

Be patient, as mastering a song takes time. And always, always warm up before belting out those high notes.. Besides improving your vocal skills, you can meet lots of new people. Plus, the thrill of performing, the joy of making music together, and the undeniable mental health benefits of singing are all part of the package. Dust off your vocal cords, get ready to embrace the scales, and step into the spotlight. The choir is calling, and it's time for you to answer with a resounding, tuneful 'yes'!

Join a local folk group

Contemplating an escape from the mainstream music scene to embrace the charming authenticity of folk tunes?

Sounds like a plan! Joining a local folk group can be a delightful journey for music lovers of all levels. Whether you're an amateur strumming your first chords or a seasoned musician, folk groups generally offer a welcoming space for everyone. Usually, you're just required to have a love for music and a willingness to learn.

Now, let's talk about expectations. Picture evenings filled with music that tells stories, gatherings where the sound of the guitar meets the rhythm of the tambourine, and where the harmonica melodiously weaves its magic. Remember, practice makes perfect, so don't fret if you don't get the chords right immediately. And yes, always be open to trying different instruments – you might discover a hidden talent!

Joining a local folk group is like finding a musical home. Not only does it hone your musical skills and understanding of folk music, but you become part of a community of like-minded individuals. There's something truly special about creating and sharing music that resonates with people on a deeply personal level. Ready to make your mark in the folk music scene? Go ahead, tune your instruments and let the folk tales flow through your music. This is your call to the world of heartfelt melodies and soul-stirring tunes!

Join a musical society

Got a burning desire to belt out show tunes while striking a dramatic pose?

Well, buckle up because joining a local musical society as a singer/actor could be your perfect gig! Whether you're a shower singer who's ready to take the next step, or a seasoned performer who's walked the boards more times than you can count, there's a spot waiting for you. No need for Broadway credentials here, just an eagerness to sing, act and make some lifelong friends.

Now, let's set the stage for your expectations. You'll be part of an ensemble that comes together to put on an annual stage show – and what a thrilling ride it is! This journey will take you from read-throughs to dress rehearsals, learning lines, and hitting those high notes.
Quick tip: stay hydrated and keep those vocal cords healthy!

It's not all work, though, being part of a musical society is akin to joining a big, happy, melodious family. You'll not only improve your performance skills but also learn the art of teamwork, discipline, and resilience. And let's not forget the adrenaline rush of applause on the closing night! So, are you ready to swap that hairbrush microphone for a real spotlight? Step out of the wings, take a deep breath, and let your talent shine in your local musical society!

Gardening superstar

Have you ever heard of the saying, "Gardening is cheaper than therapy, and you get tomatoes?"

Well, let's dig a little deeper and see why exactly so many people love gardening.

First of all, you don't need to own acres of land to enjoy gardening. Some pots on a kitchen windowsill or balcony can yield a surprisingly plentiful harvest. Urban gardening is quite the trend, and vertical gardens can turn even the tiniest space into a green paradise.

Gardening is a great way to get some outdoor exercise. It's basically a gym membership where the only 'weights' you're lifting are bags of compost or watering cans. And you can enjoy the sunshine and fresh air - bonus! Don't worry about the changing seasons either.

With a little work you can have a garden that gives you joy all year round.

Spring bulbs, summer flowers, autumn fruits and winter evergreens - your garden can be a feast for the eyes in every season.

And then there's the sense of achievement. There's nothing quite like watching a seed you've planted grow into a beautiful plant or eating a vegetable you've grown yourself. It's the kind of satisfaction that money just can't buy. Gardening also has incredible therapeutic benefits. It's a great stress reliever and can help improve mental health. There's something innately calming about being in nature, and gardening allows you to connect with the earth on a very personal level.

So, ready to trade your remote control for a rake? Don't forget, the best time to plant a garden is now! Happy gardening!

Winter gardening

Whoever said that gardening was a summer activity never heard of winter warriors, I often say to the roses in my backyard. Here are some things you can do in your garden during winter, both indoor and outdoor, because the colder months don't mean your green thumb has to hibernate.

Winter Pruning

Late winter is a perfect time for pruning many trees and shrubs. The leafless branches give you a clear view of your plant's structure and let you make precise cuts. Just make sure your shears are sharp and clean to avoid damaging your plants.

Indoor Herb Garden

Convert your kitchen into a herb paradise. Basil, parsley, cilantro, and chives are all herbs that grow well indoors. Use a sunny windowsill or invest in a grow light, and you'll have fresh herbs all winter long.

Winter Sowing

Believe it or not, you can sow seeds in the winter for a jump-start on spring and summer growing seasons. Hardy annuals, perennials, and cold vegetables (like spinach) can withstand the chilly weather.

Plant Winter-Blooming Flowers

Some plants bloom in winter, brightening your garden with color during the bleakest months. Look for pansies, hellebores, or winter jasmine.

Plan Your Spring Garden

Winter is the perfect time to plan for the spring. Enjoy a hot cup of cocoa, pull out the seed catalogs (or browse online) and start dreaming about what you'll plant when the weather warms.

You can buy plants and equipment at local nurseries, garden centers, and online stores. Always support local businesses when you can. And remember, no matter how cold it gets outside, keep your love for gardening burning!

Spring gardening

"I do love the smell of fresh mulch in the morning," I tell my petunias as spring arrives. It's time to roll up your sleeves and dig into that garden of yours! Let's look at what you can get started on in your garden during the much-anticipated spring season.

Spring Cleaning

Get your garden in shape by raking up fallen leaves, twigs, and debris. Prune away dead and damaged branches. Clear the way for fresh blooms to have their time in the sun.

Revitalize the Soil

Winter can take a toll on your garden's soil. Add organic material like compost or well-rotted manure to give it a nutritional boost. A handy soil test kit can tell you the pH level and what to add to your soil for a perfect balance.

Plant Spring Blooms

Daffodils, tulips, crocuses! Oh my! Now's the time to plant these colorful flowers. Just imagine your garden transformed into a painter's palette of vibrant colors.

Start a Veggie Patch

If you've always dreamt of picking fresh tomatoes, peppers, or zucchini right from your backyard, now's your chance.

Warm-season veggies can be started from seeds indoors and transplanted outside when the soil warms up.

Mulching

Mulch suppresses weeds, conserves soil moisture and gives your garden a neat, tidy appearance. Apply around the base of plants but not touching the stems to prevent rot.

As for purchasing plants or equipment, check out your local garden center or farmers market. They usually stock a wide variety of plants suitable for the local climate and can provide useful advice. Remember, spring is nature's way of saying, "Let's party!" So get out there and garden!

Summer gardening

"Sun's out, thumbs out!" That's the green thumb, of course! As the temperatures rise, your garden becomes the star of the show. Here are some ideas on what you can do in your garden during the sunny summer season.

Water Wisely

Summer heat can be tough on plants. Water them early in the morning or late in the evening when the sun's rays aren't as strong. This prevents water from evaporating quickly and ensures it reaches the roots.

Weed Control

Weeds love summer too, unfortunately. They compete with your plants for water and nutrients. Regularly hoe or hand-pull them, especially after a rain when the soil is soft.

Deadhead Flowers

Deadheading, or removing spent flowers, encourages plants to produce more blooms. Plus, it keeps your garden looking neat and tidy.

Harvest Time

If you've planted veggies or fruits, most likely it's time to reap the rewards! Harvest in the morning when the temperature is cooler, and the produce is crisper.

Plan for Fall

Believe it or not, late summer is the time to start thinking about your fall garden. Plant late-season crops and fall-blooming flowers.

Always wear a hat and sunscreen while gardening, because the only thing you want sizzling this summer is your barbecue, not your skin!

Fall & autumn gardening

Leaf it to Fall! That's right, autumn is the time to 'fall' back in love with your garden. As the leaves change and temperatures drop, your garden transitions into a new phase.

Here are some ideas to get you started in your garden during the cozy autumn season.

Leaf Composting

Fall provides the perfect ingredients for composting - leaves! Don't burn or bag them, compost them instead. They'll break down and provide nutrient-rich soil for next year's planting.

Plant Bulbs

For a burst of color next spring, plant bulbs like tulips and daffodils in the fall. They need a period of cold dormancy to bloom in the spring.

Autumn Pruning

Some plants benefit from being pruned in the fall. It helps to prevent disease spread and encourages healthier growth in the spring.

Indoor Gardening

As outdoor gardening winds down, indoor gardening heats up! Consider starting an indoor herb garden or nurturing houseplants.

Winter Prep

Prepare your garden for winter. Clean up debris, protect delicate plants, and mulch around trees and shrubs.

When it comes to indoor gardening, a sunny window is your best friend. Most herbs and houseplants thrive in bright, indirect light. And remember, overwatering is a common mistake with indoor plants. Wait until the top layer of soil is dry before watering again. Now, go on and 'fall' into gardening, indoors and out!

Cooking & food

Cooking classes

Are you tired of your smoke alarm being your dinner bell? Well, let's whip your culinary skills into shape! Taking cooking classes is about more than just learning to make fancy dishes. Let me explain...

Cooking classes can bolster your confidence in the kitchen. As you gain more understanding of techniques and ingredients, you'll find yourself more willing to experiment and trust your instincts. It's one thing to know you should eat healthily, it's another to know how to cook healthy meals that taste good.

Cooking classes often cover nutritional information and teach you how to create balanced meals.

Cooking classes can also introduce you to new flavors and cuisines. This not only makes cooking more exciting but also expands your culinary horizons. Understanding how to handle knives and operate kitchen equipment safely is also an underrated but crucial part of cooking. Plus when you can cook delicious meals at home, dining out becomes less of a necessity and more of a treat. And save you money!

As for skills, you don't need to be a master chef to take a cooking class. In fact, beginners are often the most frequent attendees.

Come with an open mind and a willingness to learn, and remember: in the kitchen it's okay to make a mess! So put on that apron, grab a spatula, and let's turn that smoke alarm back into a safety device! Here are some types of cooking classes you might consider:

Basic Cooking Techniques

This is a good starting point if you're a novice in the kitchen. These classes cover fundamental skills like chopping, sautéing, baking, and grilling. You'll learn the basics of cooking and gain confidence in the kitchen.

Baking and Pastry Classes

If you've got a sweet tooth, these classes are for you. They cover everything from cakes and cookies to pastries and bread. You'll learn about the science behind baking, which is quite different from cooking.

International Cuisine

Broaden your culinary horizons by exploring the cooking styles and flavors of different countries. Whether it's Italian, Mexican, French, Indian, or Thai, each cuisine offers unique techniques and ingredients that will expand your culinary repertoire.

Vegetarian/Vegan Cooking

With more people adopting plant-based diets, there's been a surge in classes focused on vegetarian and vegan cooking. These classes can teach you to create delicious, balanced meals without any animal products.

Specialty Cooking Classes

From sushi making to pizza crafting, barbecue to seafood, there's a specialty class for just about every food category you can think of.

Benefits of learning to cook different types of cuisines include a more diverse palette, understanding of different food cultures, and the ability to create a wider variety of meals.

As for skills needed to start, most cooking classes cater to all skill levels. So whether you're a master in the making or a culinary catastrophe, there's a cooking class that's just right for you.

Wine tasting

Remember, wine tasting isn't just about getting tipsy, it's about appreciating the subtle art that goes into each bottle! Wine tasting is an enjoyable activity for anyone interested in learning about wine varieties, their origins, and how to discern flavors and notes.

It's an opportunity to experience wines from various regions, grape varieties, and winemaking styles.

When you attend a wine tasting, you can expect to sample a selection of wines, typically starting with lighter wines and progressing to heavier or sweeter ones. You'll learn how to properly examine wine's color, aroma, and taste. You'll also learn about the pairing of wines with different foods.

The main tip for wine tasting is to keep an open mind. Don't worry about using 'sophisticated' wine language – just describe what you taste in your own words. And remember, you don't have to drink every drop! It's okay to spit out the wine after tasting, especially if you're sampling several wines. You'll soon expand your palate, gain knowledge about wine, and it's a great social activity.

Plus, it provides a perfect excuse to try those wines you've been eyeing in the store! Just remember, it's all about savoring and understanding, not chugging!

Travel for food

Consider a food-themed holiday if your idea of a souvenir is a delicious recipe instead of a fridge magnet! Food-themed holidays are perfect for food enthusiasts, culinary explorers, and anyone with an adventurous palate. On these trips, you can expect to taste local cuisine, learn about the food culture of the area, and perhaps even partake in cooking classes. When planning, it's essential to research the food scene of your chosen destination.

Look for local food markets, renowned eateries, and unique regional dishes. It's also beneficial to learn a few phrases in the local language to communicate dietary restrictions or preferences.

Some useful tips: don't be afraid to try something new, bring a good appetite, and remember, street food can often provide some of the most authentic and memorable culinary experiences.

You'll deepen your understanding of a place through its food, create mouth-watering memories, and, who knows, you might discover your new favorite dish. So, pack your stretchy pants and let your taste buds lead the way! Here are five great ideas for countries to visit for your next food holiday!

Italy

Italy is a food lover's paradise, famous for its pasta, pizza, gelato, and wine. Each region boasts its unique dishes like Neapolitan pizza in Naples and Pesto Genovese in Liguria. Visit during spring (April to June) or fall (September and October) for fine weather, and less tourists. Useful tip: Italians take their food etiquette seriously; remember to enjoy your meals leisurely and don't ask for extra cheese unless offered!

Thailand

Known for its street food, Thailand offers an explosion of flavors with dishes like Pad Thai, Green Curry, and Mango Sticky Rice.

Visit between November and February when the weather is cool and dry. Remember, Thai food can be quite spicy, so be sure to communicate your spice tolerance to your server!

France

France, particularly Paris, is synonymous with culinary excellence. From escargot and coq au vin to croissants and macarons, French cuisine is diverse and sophisticated. Visit during spring (April to June) or fall (September to November). Useful tip: French dining is an experience, so don't rush your meal. And don't forget to pair your food with some fine French wine!

Japan

Japan offers an exquisite culinary journey, with dishes like sushi, ramen, and tempura. Don't miss the unique experience of a traditional Kaiseki meal. Visit during spring (March to May) for cherry blossom season or autumn (September to November) for fall colors. Useful tip: Be respectful of Japanese dining etiquette, which includes not sticking your chopsticks upright in a bowl of rice.

Mexico

Mexican cuisine goes beyond tacos and nachos. Each region has its unique dishes, like mole in Oaxaca and ceviche on the coasts.

The dry season, between December and April, is the best time to visit. Useful tip: Street food is a vital part of Mexican food culture, so be adventurous and try the local markets and street vendors!

Home brewing

Whoever said patience is a virtue probably had a homebrewer in mind!

Home brewing is for anyone who has a love for beer and a bit of a do-it-yourself spirit. As a home brewer, you'll take on the fascinating process of turning water, malt, hops, and yeast into your very own beer. It might seem complex at first, but with a bit of practice, you'll be crafting ales, lagers, or stouts that can rival your favorite brands.

A useful tip is to always keep everything clean; sanitation is critical in brewing to avoid unwanted flavors.

You get to understand the brewing process intimately, create your own unique beer recipes, and of course, impress your friends with your brewmaster skills. Plus, there's a deep sense of satisfaction in enjoying a beer that you made yourself. Starter kits are available online, and local homebrew supply shops often offer classes. Cheers to that!

Animals

Adopt an animal

Thinking of adopting a cat or dog? Congratulations, you're about to experience a new level of love and furry chaos! Adopting a pet is a wonderful decision that can bring joy, companionship, and a touch of mayhem into anyone's life.

Adopting a cat or dog from a shelter can be an incredibly rewarding experience. These animals often come from challenging backgrounds and providing them with a loving home can drastically improve their quality of life. Plus, by adopting, you're not supporting potential puppy or kitten mills, where animals can be bred in inhumane conditions for profit.

Furthermore, adoption usually includes vaccinations, spaying or neutering, and microchipping in the adoption fee. Shelters and rescues also have a wide variety of breeds and ages, meaning you can find the perfect companion to match your lifestyle. Most importantly, by choosing to adopt, you're saving a life and making room for another animal in need at the shelter.

Adopting a pet isn't all about cute Instagram photos and cuddle sessions, it's like signing up for a marathon of responsibility and commitment! Adopting a dog or cat means taking on the responsibility of another life and it's not a decision to be taken lightly.

These animals require daily care, including feeding, grooming, and most importantly, your time and attention.

They need social interaction and mental stimulation to lead happy lives, so playing with them and keeping them engaged is crucial. Leaving them alone for extended periods can lead to anxiety and behavioral issues. Dogs, in particular, need regular exercise, and certain breeds may require more than others. A good rule of thumb is a walk every day, but remember, a tired dog is a happy dog! Regular vet visits are also a must to keep up with vaccinations and monitor their overall health. Adopting an animal is a commitment that will likely last a decade or more. It's not just about providing them with a home, but also a loving family. If you're not ready for the marathon, perhaps wait until you're ready to go the distance. But if you are ready, you will have an incredible journey of love and companionship!

Before you adopt, ensure you have the basics: a food and water dish, a comfy bed, toys, pet food, a collar and leash for a dog, or a litter box for a cat. Expect a period of adjustment as your new pet gets used to their surroundings. They may be a bit shy or anxious at first but with patience, they will understand that they are in a loving home. A crucial tip is to schedule a vet visit soon after adoption to check on their health and start a vaccination schedule. Prepare your home by pet-proofing it - secure loose wires, keep harmful substances out of reach, and provide safe spaces for them to rest. Remember, adopting a pet is a lifelong commitment but the purrs, wagging tails, and unconditional love make it all worth it!

Train a guide dog puppy

Choosing to provide a loving home and help train a guide dog puppy is a noble and fulfilling task. This role is crucial in preparing the young dogs for their future as invaluable companions to people who are visually impaired or have other disabilities. You can expect to teach the puppy basic commands, socialization skills, and some specific tasks that will aid their future partner. Remember, patience is key – these puppies are young and eager to learn, but they're still puppies. Regular positive reinforcement and consistency are vital in training. Be prepared for the emotional attachment you'll undoubtedly form with your furry trainee.

After about a year, the puppy will move on to advanced training and eventually, to their forever home. Although saying goodbye can be tough, the knowledge that you've played an integral part in the puppy's journey to becoming a life-changing companion for someone in need is incredibly rewarding.

Volunteer at local animal shelter

Picture it: a chorus of wagging tails and purring faces, all ecstatic to see you. Now, that's a volunteering job worth signing up for!

Volunteering at a local animal shelter is a rewarding experience that can be life changing for both you and the animals.

It's perfect for animal lovers who may not have the time or resources for a pet of their own, or anyone wanting to give back to their community. Expect duties like feeding, cleaning, walking dogs, and socializing with the animals. It's important to remember that while it's full of cute, cuddly moments, it can also be physically demanding and emotionally challenging, especially when dealing with animals who've had tough pasts.

Wear comfortable clothes that you don't mind getting a little dirty, and bringing a positive, patient attitude. The benefits are plentiful: besides the obvious joy of spending time with animals, you'll also be helping them to socialize, thus increasing their chances of adoption.

You can also learn about different breeds and their behaviors, and you might even find your new best friend! So, pull on your rubber gloves, prepare for some puppy kisses, and step into a world of unconditional love and tail wags.

Take horseback riding lessons

Starting horse riding lessons is an adventure that combines physical activity with an exceptional opportunity to connect with these majestic creatures.

Perfect for all age groups, these lessons can be tailored to each individual's comfort and skill level.

Expect to learn basics like mounting, dismounting and communicating with your horse in the saddle.

You will also learn more advanced techniques such as trotting, cantering, and jumping as you progress.

A key part of your training will involve natural horsemanship techniques, which emphasize understanding and working with a horse's instincts and communication cues, forging a deep bond of trust and respect. Tips for beginners include wearing appropriate gear (like a good helmet and sturdy boots), listening to your instructor, and maintaining patience and calmness around the horses. You'll enjoy better physical fitness, enhanced coordination and balance, and boosted confidence.

Not to mention, the therapeutic effects of being around horses are well-documented, with numerous studies highlighting their role in reducing stress and promoting mental well-being. So, saddle up and prepare for an unforgettable journey of learning, growth, and equine friendship!

Get political

Politics isn't all just debates, speeches, and heated arguments. It's also about community, connection, and making a difference! Joining your local political party is a great way to get involved in your community and have a direct impact on major decisions that will affect your community.

It's open to anyone with a passion for change, irrespective of your background or experience. Expect to participate in local meetings, assist in election campaigns, volunteer for community events, and even run for office if you're feeling ambitious. You'll learn a lot about how the government works, from local regulations to national legislation.

This experience can be incredibly fulfilling and enlightening, helping you understand the intricacies of the political landscape. A tip for newcomers is to be open-minded and willing to listen to various perspectives, even if they differ from your own. It's also essential to be proactive, taking the initiative to volunteer for tasks and propose new ideas.

The benefits of joining a local political party extend beyond the political sphere. You'll develop valuable skills such as public speaking, negotiation, and leadership. Moreover, you'll build a network of like-minded individuals who could become lifelong friends. So, if you've ever thought, 'I wish they'd do something about that!', here's your chance to be the 'they' and do something about it!

Further education & getting on stage

Local college courses

Taking a part-time or evening course can be really good for you. It helps you learn new things while still having time for work or other stuff during the day. You might find courses in things like cooking, computer skills, languages, or even fun hobbies like painting. You can expect to learn at a slower pace, which is great if you like to take your time. The best tip is to choose a course you're excited about. That way, it'll be easier to stay motivated. And remember, learning new things is important no matter how old we get. It keeps our brains sharp and makes life more interesting.

Languages

Why pay for an expensive plane ticket to study to learn a new language abroad, when you can learn a new language using an app in your living room or joining a local evening class? That's the beauty of taking a part-time or evening course to learn a new language! It's perfect for busy bees who want to add some spice to their skill set without disturbing their daily routine. Whether you want to say "Bonjour" in French, "Hola" in Spanish, or "Ni hao" in Mandarin, there's a course out there for you. You can expect to meet like-minded language enthusiasts, delve into new cultures, and sometimes, even get a bit tongue-tied - but that's all part of the fun! A tip from the wise: consistency is key.

Practice a little every day, and don't be shy to make mistakes. Remember, fluency isn't built in a day. So, dust off that old notebook, charge up those headphones, and get ready to explore the world, one language at a time!

Spanish

With over 460 million native speakers worldwide, Spanish tops the chart of popular languages to learn. It's not only the official language in 21 countries, but it's also widely spoken in the US. Learning Spanish can open doors to new job opportunities, fascinating cultures, and exotic travel destinations. To practice, try watching Spanish films or listening to Spanish music.

Mandarin Chinese

Mandarin Chinese is the most spoken language in the world, and is incredibly useful, especially in business contexts. It might seem intimidating with its complex characters, but once you start to figure it out, you'll be communicating with over a billion people! Flashcards are great for learning characters, and Chinese podcasts can help with pronunciation.

French

French is spoken in over 29 countries. It's also a working language of the United Nations. Learning French can enhance your appreciation for French cuisine, cinema, and literature. Try reading French books or newspapers to improve your vocabulary.

German

German is a great asset for anyone interested in European history, philosophy, or business. Practice by watching German movies with subtitles, or try your hand at writing simple sentences in German.

Arabic

Arabic is widely spoken in the Middle East and North Africa. It's increasingly important in international diplomacy and business. Arabic calligraphy is a beautiful art form you can explore as you learn. Learning a new language has numerous benefits, from boosting cognitive abilities to opening up a world of new friendships and experiences.

A useful tip for language learning is to immerse yourself as much as possible. Use language learning apps, join language exchange groups, and don't shy away from speaking, even if you make mistakes.

When you're abroad, the best way to practice your new language is to use it in everyday situations. Order food in a restaurant, ask for directions, or talk to a local. Remember, the key is to practice regularly and be patient with yourself.

Conferences

If you're picturing a room full of people dozing off during a dull PowerPoint presentation, think again!

Today's educational conferences are vibrant, interactive spaces where learning, networking, and innovation go hand in hand. These events, spanning from technology to gardening, are treasure troves of knowledge, delivered by experts in the field. They offer you the chance to broaden your horizons, learn new skills, and connect with like-minded individuals. So whether you're a conference newbie or a seasoned attendee, buckle up! Here are some popular event types:

Crafting conventions offer a plethora of workshops and exhibits for various crafts. They're useful for learning new crafting techniques, discovering supplies and tools, and meeting fellow crafters.

Board game conventions are great for game enthusiasts to discover new games, participate in tournaments, and meet game designers. They're beneficial for expanding your game collection, learning about game design, and connecting with fellow gamers.

Writing conferences are great platforms for aspiring writers to learn from established authors, attend insightful workshops, and even pitch to agents. They're useful for honing your craft, getting inspired, and understanding the publishing landscape.

Marketing events offer valuable insights into the latest marketing trends, strategies, and tools.

They're beneficial for staying ahead of the curve, networking with industry professionals, and gaining actionable ideas to boost your business.

Entrepreneurship events provide aspiring entrepreneurs with the opportunity to learn from successful business leaders, find potential investors, and network with other startups. They're useful for gaining practical business insights, getting motivated, and building valuable connections.

Photography conferences offer great learning opportunities for both amateur and professional photographers.

These events often feature workshops, photo walks, and talks from experts in the field, making them useful for improving your skills, learning about the latest gear, and networking with fellow photography enthusiasts.

Gardening events offer garden lovers a wealth of knowledge about plant care, landscape design, and sustainable practices. They're beneficial for discovering new plant species, learning innovative gardening techniques, and connecting with other green thumbs.

Culinary conferences are perfect for foodies and aspiring chefs.

They offer a chance to learn new recipes, watch cooking demonstrations, and taste dishes from renowned chefs. They're useful for expanding your culinary repertoire and networking with food industry professionals.

Fitness conventions offer workshops, training sessions, and product expos. You can learn about the latest fitness trends, techniques, and equipment. They're beneficial for enhancing your fitness routine, getting motivated, and connecting with fitness professionals.

Remember to plan your days in advance. Look at the schedule and highlight the workshops or speakers you're interested in.

Bring a notebook or device for note-taking, and don't forget your camera or phone for capturing moments and business cards for networking. You can find these conferences through online search engines, hobby forums, or social media groups related to your interest. Event websites may also list such conferences.

The benefits of attending conferences are plenty: learning from experts, keeping up with trends, networking, and even finding new hobbies or interests. Remember, active participation is key, so ask questions, engage with others, and most importantly, enjoy the experience!

Acting

Embarking on an acting journey can feel a bit like stepping onto a stage with no script; exciting, but a tad intimidating! To start with, consider taking acting classes. Schools, community centers, or local theaters often offer them. Event websites can help you find classes or acting communities in your area.

These classes usually cover a range of topics like improvisation, character development, and voice training. They're beneficial not only for learning acting techniques but also for boosting your confidence and communication skills. Acting can also be therapeutic, as it encourages self-expression and empathy.

Joining a local acting community or theater group is another great step. You can meet fellow aspiring actors, learn from their experiences, and even participate in group performances.

Once you're ready to get on stage, remember that preparation is key. Know your script inside out and understand your character's motivations. Practice in front of a mirror or video yourself to identify areas you can improve.

When it's time for the actual performance, nerves are normal. Use them as fuel for your performance. Warm up your body and voice before going on stage. And most importantly, enjoy the process! Acting is about living in the moment and conveying genuine emotion.

Also, be open to feedback. It's an integral part of the learning process. Expect a mix of highs and lows – standing ovations one day, forgotten lines the next. But don't get discouraged. Every actor, no matter how successful, has had their share of stumbles.

Audition for local plays, student films, or even commercials. Create a portfolio or show reel showcasing your performances. And remember, acting is not just about talent; it's about perseverance, resilience, and a love for the craft. So step into the spotlight, and let your journey begin!

Stand up comedy

The world of stand-up comedy is a thrilling roller coaster ride of laughs, applause, and yes, sometimes even awkward silence.

But fear not, every comedian starts somewhere. To begin with, consider enrolling in a stand-up comedy class. Schools and community centers may offer them, or you could explore online courses too.

These classes can help you understand the basics of joke writing, comedic timing, and stage presence. They also offer a safe space to try out your material and get constructive feedback. The benefits of stand-up comedy extend beyond the stage too. It can boost your confidence, enhance your public speaking skills, and offer a creative outlet for self-expression.

Finding a local comedy community or open mic night is a great way to immerse yourself in the stand-up scene. Local event listings can help you find these. Attending these events can give you a sense of different comedic styles and what kind of humor resonates with audiences.

When you're ready to step on stage, preparation is crucial. Craft a set that's true to your voice and perspective. Keep it concise, especially if you're performing at an open mic night where time is limited. Practice your set repeatedly, paying attention to your timing and delivery.

Your first time on stage might be nerve-racking, but remember, even the best comedians have bombed at some point.

Expect a mix of reactions. Some jokes might have the audience in stitches, others might be met with crickets. Don't let this discourage you. Every performance is a learning opportunity. Listen to your audience. If a joke consistently doesn't land, consider reworking it. Record your performances to review later, and be open to feedback. Network with other comedians and learn from their experiences. Most importantly, enjoy the process. Stand-up comedy is about making people laugh and having fun doing it. So grab that microphone, take a deep breath, and let your comedic journey begin!

Map your family tree

Mapping your family tree can be a fascinating journey into your past, unveiling stories of ancestors and tracing lineage far and wide. The benefits of this exploration extend beyond mere curiosity; it can help you understand your family's health history, discover long-lost relatives, or simply appreciate your heritage more deeply.

To begin, start with what you know. List down your immediate family members and then gradually move to your grandparents, great-grandparents, and so on. Put together any information you have, such as names, birthplaces, dates of birth, death, and marriage.

Family gatherings, photo albums, letters, and official documents like birth certificates or census records can be valuable resources in this process.

Next, choose a way to organize your information. You could use a simple notebook or a spreadsheet, or specialized software and online platforms which offer detailed templates and tools for constructing your family tree.

If you're struggling to find information, consider taking a DNA test.. This can provide clues about your ancestry and even connect you with distant relatives. Remember that privacy is a concern with such tests, so do your research before deciding to take one.

Expect the process to be a bit like a detective game.

Some information will come easily, while other connections might require a lot of digging. You might hit dead ends or discover surprising facts. Be patient and persistent.

Reach out to elder family members for stories and information. Not only can this fill gaps in your tree, but it will also preserve family memories. Lastly, always verify the information you find. It's easy to mix up people with the same name, or get dates confused. Cross-check facts where possible.

Mapping your family tree is a unique adventure, a personal exploration into your roots. It might be time-consuming, but the discoveries and connections you make along the way make it worthwhile.

So, grab a pen, start asking questions, and let your family history unfold!

Volunteering & mentoring

If you've ever thought about trading your online video subscription for something a little more fulfilling, then volunteering or mentoring in your local community might be your ticket to satisfaction! Whether you're tutoring students at the neighborhood school, serving meals at a local soup kitchen, or guiding a young person through life's ups and downs, volunteering offers countless opportunities to make a difference. But the benefits aren't just one-sided. As you pour into your community, you'll also discover new skills, meet diverse people, and experience the deep fulfillment that comes from giving back. However, there's more to volunteering than simply showing up.

From understanding what's expected of you, to choosing the right opportunity that matches your interests and availability, there's a fair bit to consider. So, whether you're new to volunteering or a seasoned pro looking to explore different opportunities, let's dive into the rewarding world of community service and mentorship!

Local Schools

You can offer to tutor students in subjects you're good at, assist teachers, or even run after-school programs or sports coaching. This can be a great experience as you help shape young minds and contribute to their academic growth.

Senior Centers

Many senior centers appreciate volunteers to help with daily activities, offer companionship to the elderly, or share a skill like teaching a computer class. This provides a sense of community and connection for older adults and can be a deeply enriching experience.

Community Centers

These hubs often need volunteers for various activities, from organizing events to teaching classes or workshops. You can share your talents and interests with your community.

Food Banks and Soup Kitchens

Volunteering at these places involves tasks like preparing meals, organizing food drives, or distributing food. This is a direct way to help those facing food insecurity in your community.

Animal Shelters

Animal shelters always need helping hands for tasks like feeding animals, cleaning cages, or walking dogs. If you're an animal lover, this is a rewarding way to spend your time.

Local Parks and Gardens

Many parks and gardens need volunteers for maintaining trails, planting trees, or leading nature walks.

This is perfect for those who love the outdoors and environmental conservation.

Libraries

Libraries often seek volunteers to help with book sorting, running events, or literacy programs. If you're a bookworm, this could be the perfect fit for you.

Mentorship Programs

Local youth centers often look for mentors to provide guidance and support to young people. As a mentor, you can make a significant impact on a young person's life.

Volunteering and mentoring in your local community can offer numerous benefits, including the joy of giving back, the opportunity to develop new skills, and the chance to meet like-minded individuals. You'll need to agree to a certain amount of time and energy to your chosen activity. Always choose something that aligns with your interests and schedule. Before you start, understand the requirements of the role you're taking on. Be reliable, respectful, and open-minded. Remember, the aim is to make a positive contribution to your community. The experience can be as rewarding for you as it is beneficial for your community!

Charity work

Rolling up your sleeves and diving into charity work in your local community is like turning the channel from a drama series to a feel-good movie, it just leaves you with a warm, fuzzy feeling inside! Whether it's organizing a fundraising event, helping out at a local food bank, or even starting your own charitable initiative, there are countless ways you can make a positive impact. And the benefits aren't just for your community, they're for you too. You'll not only discover new skills and meet inspiring people, but you'll also experience the joy that comes from helping others. But before you leap into action, there are some things to consider. Understanding the commitment involved, aligning your passions with your actions, and knowing how to maximize your impact are all part of the journey. Whether you're a first-time volunteer or a seasoned charitable champion, let's explore the meaningful and rewarding world of local charity work together!

Food Banks and Soup Kitchens

Volunteering here involves tasks like preparing meals, packing food parcels, or even organizing food drives. This direct method of charity work helps those facing food insecurity, offering immediate aid to those in need.

Community Clean-Up

Organize or join clean-up drives in your local parks, beaches, or neighborhoods.

It's a great way to contribute to environmental conservation and instill a sense of pride in your community.

Charity Runs or Walks

Participate in or help organize charity runs or walks. These events often raise funds for specific causes, and your involvement can make a big difference.

Homeless Shelters

These facilities always need volunteers for various tasks, from serving meals to providing companionship or skills training. This work directly benefits those experiencing homelessness in your community.

Hospitals and Care Homes

Many hospitals and care homes welcome volunteers to interact with patients, read to them, or help with basic tasks. This can significantly improve the patients' day-to-day experience.

Fundraising Events

Host a fundraising event like a garage sale, bake sale, or benefit concert. The funds raised can go to a local charity of your choice.

Donate Blood or Organize a Blood Drive

This is a life-saving act of charity that directly benefits individuals in critical need of blood donations.

Charity work in your local community offers numerous benefits, such as the satisfaction of giving back, learning new skills, and making new friendships. Plus, it helps foster a stronger, more connected community. Expect to commit time and effort to your chosen cause, and remember to choose something that aligns with your interests and values. Understand the requirements and expectations of your role, be reliable, and keep an open mind.

Before starting any charity work, it's a good idea to research the cause or organization you're interested in to make sure they share with your values and goals.

Be sure to respect the dignity and privacy of those you're helping, and always be open to learning from your experiences. In the end, the success of your charity work will not only be measured by the difference you make in your community but also the growth and fulfillment you experience along the way.

Entrepreneurship adventures

Buckle up, aspiring entrepreneur, because starting a new business is a bit like strapping into a rollercoaster - it's thrilling, a little scary, and full of unexpected twists and turns! But don't worry, because just like a rollercoaster, it can be the ride of a lifetime.

Launching your own business comes with a host of benefits, from the freedom to pursue your passion, to the satisfaction of creating something truly your own. However, it also involves challenges, like long hours, tough decisions, and the risk of failure. But don't be daunted; every successful entrepreneur has been in your shoes. With determination and a clear vision you'll be well on your way to turning your dream into reality. Whether you're still mulling over that innovative idea or ready to take the entrepreneurial plunge, let's see what your options are!

Online business ideas

Starting an online business comes with numerous benefits, such as flexibility, low startup costs, and the potential to reach a global audience. However, it also requires dedication, patience, and a willingness to adapt and learn. Here are some ideas to consider:

Blogging

If you enjoy writing and a unique perspective on a particular topic, starting a blog can be a great idea. You can earn revenue through advertising, sponsored posts, or selling products and services.

eCommerce Store

Platforms like Shopify or Etsy make it easy to start selling products online. This could be anything from handmade crafts, vintage items, or even digital products like eBooks or design templates.

Online Courses and Coaching

If you're an expert in a specific field, consider creating online courses or offering coaching services. Websites like Udemy or Teachable make it easy to host and sell your courses.

Affiliate Marketing

This involves promoting other companies' products and earning a commission for each sale made.

Make a website or start a social media channel focused on a specific niche.

Freelance Writing, Design, or Programming

Online platforms connect freelancers with clients who need services. If you have a skill like writing, graphic design, or coding, this could be a viable business option.

Social Media Consulting

If you're savvy with social media platforms and understand how to build online followings, consider offering social media consulting services to businesses.

Virtual Assistant Services

Many businesses and individuals are willing to outsource administrative tasks to virtual assistants. This can include anything from managing emails and schedules to handling customer service.

Stock Photography

If you're a skilled photographer, consider selling your photos as stock images.

Turning your hobby into a business

Turning your hobbies into a business is all about finding what you love doing and then finding a way to add value for others. For instance, if you enjoy baking, you could start a business selling homemade baked goods online.

Craft Making

If you love crafting, consider selling your handmade items on online platforms. From jewelry and candles to knitted items and custom stationery, there's a market for unique, artisanal products.

Baking or Cooking

Turn your culinary skills into a catering or bakery business. You can sell to friends and family, at local events, or even online.

Photography

If you have a talent for taking photos, consider starting a photography business.

You can specialize in weddings, portraits, product photography, or sell your images as stock photos.

Writing

Passionate writers can start a blog, offer freelance writing services, or even write and self-publish a book. You can monetize your writing through selling your own products, writing adverts for others or writing sponsored posts as a job.

Fitness

If you're a fitness enthusiast, consider becoming a personal trainer or a fitness instructor. You could also create and sell workout plans online.

Gardening

Turn your green thumb into a business by selling plants, seeds, or homegrown produce. You could also start a landscaping or garden design service.

Music

Talented musicians can give music lessons, perform at events, or create and sell music online. You could also start a music-related blog or an online video channel.

Art

Artists can sell their work online, at art shows or local markets. You could also offer art lessons or share art tutorials.

Turning your hobby into a business has many benefits, such as the potential for financial gain, flexible working hours, and the satisfaction of doing what you love. However, expect challenges. Not every hobby makes a profitable business, and it requires dedication, marketing skills, and often involves long hours. Here are some tips to get started:

Market Research: Understand your target audience and competition.
Business Plan: Outline your business model, marketing strategy, and financial projections.

Pricing: Learn to price your products or services correctly, factoring in your time, materials, and overheads.

Marketing: Learn basic marketing skills to promote your business effectively.

Legalities: Ensure you comply with all relevant legal and tax requirements.

Remember, while it's exciting to turn your passion into profit, it's important to maintain the joy your hobby brings you. Don't let the pressure of business take away the fun and fulfillment of your hobby.

Expect challenges and competition. It's important to do market research, understand your audience, and define your unique selling proposition.

Remember to set realistic goals and celebrate small victories along the way. You can find lots of online resources to help you start and grow your business, including business mentoring programs, online entrepreneurship courses, and business development centers. So take that leap, follow your passion, and create something amazing!

You're a legend!

Congratulations! You've made it to the last chapter of this book. By now, you've probably tried out a few things from the list, and we hope you've made some wonderful memories along the way. But remember, the end of this book doesn't mean the end of your adventures! You, my friend, are living proof that retirement is not a full stop but an exclamation mark on life!

Have you tried wine tasting yet? Don't worry if you can't tell a Merlot from a Shiraz. The important thing is that you had fun spitting wine into a bucket in a fancy setting.

Have you ticked off everything on your bucket list yet?

Well, it's time to make a new one.

And remember, it's not about how many things you've ticked off, but the joy you've experienced while doing them.

Are you now a published author with your life's story selling like hot cakes? Fantastic! Now, how about writing a fantasy novel or a cookbook? You've got the time and the creative juices flowing, so why not?

Remember when we said 'globetrotter' would look great on your retired status? Well, it looks fabulous! So, keep exploring, keep discovering, keep adding stamps to your passport. And if you found tranquility in gardening or excitement in surfing, that's brilliant!

You've learned that retirement is about living your life the way you've always wanted to - full of laughter, learning, and a fair share of unexpected turns.

So here we are, at the end of this book, but certainly not the end of your adventures. Remember, age is just a number and you're as young as you feel. So, strap on your boots, get your gears ready, and head out for another exciting day. After all, retirement is a ride that's more rock 'n roll than rocking chair.

So, whether you're writing your next novel, planning your next vacation, or tuning your guitar for your next gig, remember this – retirement is not the end, but the beginning of the most exciting chapter of your life. Let's rock this retirement thing!

www.ingramcontent.com/pod-product-compliance
Lightning Source LLC
Chambersburg PA
CBHW030051100526
44591CB00008B/104